Successful
Assembly Automation

Successful
Assembly Automation

a development
and implementation guide

By Dean A. Shafer, PE

Society of Manufacturing Engineers
Dearborn, Michigan

Library of Congress Catalog Card Number: 98-061066
ISBN: 0-87263-499-X

Additional copies may be obtained by contacting:

Society of Manufacturing Engineers
Customer Service
One SME Drive, P.O. Box 930
Dearborn, MI 48121-0930
1-800-733-4763

SME staff who participated in producing this book:

Philip Mitchell, Handbook Editor
Rosemary Csizmadia, Production Supervisor
Kathye Quirk, Production Assistant
Frances Kania, Production Assistant

Printed in the United States of America

To Lynn, my wife and best friend,
who has always supported me in everything I've done,
and in memory of my father,
who instilled in me his interest in machines.

Acknowledgments

The author wishes to thank Mark H. Smith for contributing Chapter 8: *Controls* to this book.

The following people are also gratefully acknowledged for their help:

Jeff A. Barrett

Andrew H. Bekkala PE, Ph.D.

Edward J. Brdlik

Darrell L. Crosby

Mandel L. Desnick

Patrick M. Duerr

Gary L. Engstrom

Dr. Dennis E. Ferguson PE

Jean M. Fisher

Allan D. Hammel

Lee E. Hitzeman

Robert M. Johnson, CMfgE

Kenneth R. Kaufhold

Dave C. Kral

Alan F. Kubinski, PE

Bruce W. Livermore

Dr. Clive Loughlin

Kirk A. Mathison

Vit R. Miller

Dr. John R. Mlinar

Richard J. Offord

Kenneth L. Penttila

Steve Reiser

Frank J. Riley, CMfgE, PE

Gary W. Schukar, PE

Andre Sharon, Ph.D.

Mark H. Smith

Dale F. Snyder

Steven M. Spicer

Bruce J. Ties

Paul Winberg, PE

Contents

1 Manufacturing Theory

2 General Principles

3 Defining the Assembly Process

4 The Product

5 Assembly Processes

6 Component Feeding

7 Inspection and Measurement

8 Control Systems

9 Machine Design Considerations

10 Debug, Checkout, and Startup

Appendix A: Miscellaneous Tips

Index

Tables and Figures

Chapter 4

Chapter 5

Chapter 10

Appendix

Introduction

This book is for manufacturing and engineering personnel who make and assemble products and who want to help their organization become one of the world's best manufacturers. The first five chapters contain general information that is important to all organizational levels in the plant, such as research and development, manufacturing management, and the manufacturing engineer. Starting with Chapter 6, *Component Feeding*, the book becomes more directed at practicing engineers and designers involved in specifying, obtaining, and designing assembly equipment.

Engineers who do not routinely handle individual parts or web-fed parts can benefit greatly from learning the basic practices used by engineers with more experience in these areas. Those engineers already experienced in part handling can refine and improve their skills by learning from others with different experiences.

Designing special assembly equipment is challenging, because much of the equipment is unique to the application. Unlike a packaging machine—where the basic machine is standard and modifications are required only for the current package size—special assembly machines vary as widely as the products they assemble. Even if a "standard" machine chassis is used, the equipment quickly becomes unique to the specific assembly task. Automated assembly is higher risk than most manufacturing processes, because so much of the equipment is unique. Some attempts have been made to standardize the design approach. This can be beneficial in certain cases, for example, where using a standard machine base, transfer device, or chassis can save both time and cost. However, relying on standard approaches to automation can limit creativity. It can even put your business at a competitive disadvantage with other manufacturers who choose a more aggressive automation approach. Using the same automation approach as your competition will result in a comparable manufacturing cost structure at best.

One of this book's objectives is to take automated assembly from an art to a science. Although using "the standard approach" will probably not provide any manufacturing competitive advantage, it is unwise and unnecessary to reinvent each new assembly project. Experienced automation engineers have developed effective methods and approaches. Unfortunately, these methods and approaches were usually learned by each individual independently through experience. By documenting as many of these basics as possible, it is hoped that new automation engineers can learn the basics quickly and move on to adding to the body of knowledge.

Another objective is to provide both background and methods for managing the risks of automated assembly projects. By organizing the basic approaches to assembly and sharing the techniques of the past, the challenges of the future can be approached more systematically. Emphasis must be placed on recognizing the risks in each process step, and then managing the risks by either using a proven technique or thoroughly testing the "new ground" by prototyping, as described in Chapter 2.

Information on handling "soft" products is scarce. Most of the information currently available is aimed at the assembly of hard goods—either automotive or other hard products such as electrical components, medical devices, hardware items, and plastic assemblies. Essentially, no information can be found on handling "soft" components targeted for high-volume disposable markets. Soft components are those with very little rigidity, such as paper, film, and nonwovens. They are often handled in web form. Likewise, essentially no information can be found on assembly of products at a rate above 60 parts per minute (ppm). Competing effectively in the disposable products arena necessitates driving production rates higher whenever practical.

This book is a collection of experience and knowledge from a broad cross section of people involved in handling and assembling discrete components and soft goods. It is not a complete description of how to design and manage an automated assembly system. It is intended to fill the gap where existing literature is either inadequate or nonexistent and additional information on a subject is referenced when possible.

Product complexity and volumes vary greatly, as does the equipment to produce them. The number of components in a product can range from three for beverages (bottle, cap, and liquid) to thousands for automobiles. Equipment for bottling, canning, and other high-speed packaging operations is usually provided by suppliers specializing in this type of equipment. Bottling machines are usually continuous motion and run at hundreds, even thousands of units per minute. There are many very good suppliers of equipment for assembly of automotive and appliance products, and this type of equipment is the best documented. The equipment for these products is typically intermittent motion and usually runs in the 30 to 60 units per minute range. High-volume items, such as disposable products, are in the middle ground and are not well covered in the literature, nor are there many suppliers in this arena. This book addresses the techniques and equipment used in the manufacture of disposable products as well as automotive and appliance products. However, most of the concepts discussed will apply to any automated assembly process.

Lord Kelvin correctly stated, "When you can measure what you are speaking about, and express it in numbers, you know something about it; but when you cannot measure it . . . your knowledge is of a meager and unsatisfactory kind..." For this reason, numbers are included whenever possible. However, supplying numbers does not eliminate all disagreement. For example, putting a scale to a chart showing the relationship between the number of components and the speed of assembly is bound to generate some controversy. There are exceptions to every rule, and no two experts in any area are likely to come up with exactly the same numbers. Nevertheless, this is the best place for the novice to start, even if the numbers provided may not be exact or definitive. Please consider this when viewing the figures and tables.

As a teenager, I verbally sparred with my father about "judgment" (usually in regard to driving). Although I had a good sense that we were arguing different aspects of judgment, I enjoyed the discussion and we continued to use the term with each other as long as he was alive. I, of course, was referring to the ability to judge things like speed and distance (which I claimed a younger person could do better). He, on the other hand, was referring to the mental ability to make sound and reasonable decisions. This book describes ideals. In the real world, the ideal must be balanced with what is practical and justified. It would be naive to expect any one project to go through all the steps suggested in this book. The decision maker must use experience and judgment to determine which steps must be taken and which can be skipped. Every automation project involves trade-offs between cost, time, and risk. Hopefully, the information contained in this book will help the reader make those decisions by improving his or her understanding of the impact and risk associated with the choices. Although the young engineer with a computer can make rapid and highly accurate judgments regarding the technical aspects of a design, world-class manufacturing requires vision, experience, and a great deal of judgment—of the sound and reasonable decision type.

REFERENCE

Lord Kelvin. 1824-1907. Scottish mathematician and physicist.

1

Manufacturing Theory

MANUFACTURING GOALS

Before focusing on issues specific to automated assembly, it is useful to review some of the issues facing manufacturing in general. To develop an effective manufacturing system, it is necessary to understand the long-range goals of the manufacturing organization. Often, one goal of manufacturing is to become a "world-class manufacturer." This may be defined as being among the best in a particular industry and at least one important aspect of manufacturing (Hayes, Wheelwright, and Clark 1988). To become the "low-cost producer" or the "highest quality producer" are other frequent long-range goals of a manufacturing organization. Whatever manufacturing has established as its long-range goal, the assembly system should be developed with that goal in mind.

Shorter-term manufacturing objectives are generally more obvious. They are the justification for a current project, such as cost reduction, quality improvement, volume increase, and safety. For example, eliminating a manual operation that is causing repetitive stress injuries is increasingly used to justify automation. These are the objectives that the current project will be judged against and must be of primary concern during the development of the project. However, short-term project objectives must be consistent with long-term manufacturing goals if the business is to be competitive in the long run.

STAGES OF MANUFACTURING

There are four stages in the progression of manufacturing competitiveness: Stage I—reactive; Stage II—supportive; Stage III—contributing; and Stage IV—leading (Hayes, Wheelwright, and Clark 1988).

Stage I: Reactive

In the reactive stage, the manufacturing organization meets internal manufacturing requirements. It is neutral in the manufacturing decision making process. The goal of the organization is to meet the manufacturing needs identified by the company.

Example

Joe is in charge of manufacturing. He manufactures products that people bring to him in the way that he is instructed. New manufacturing equipment with more or different features is purchased in response to the needs expressed by others in the organization. Joe reacts to the needs of the people that use his manufacturing services.

Stage II: Supportive

During the supportive stage, the manufacturing organization stays current with external manufacturing requirements, such as the manufacturing requirements of the competition. It investigates and adopts the current standard manufacturing practices of the industry.

Example

Sue is in charge of manufacturing. She maintains her knowledge on how the competition manufactures products and recommends the best way to manufacture products to keep up with the competition. Periodically, she recommends to management the purchase of new manufacturing equipment with more or different features, to stay competitive.

Stage III: Contributing

In the contributing stage, the manufacturing organization tailors its manufacturing decisions and objectives to the competitive strategy of the business.

Example

Bill is in charge of manufacturing and maintains his knowledge on the latest manufacturing technology. He suggests to management new and creative ways that manufacturing can be done to keep up with the competition. The decision to purchase new manufacturing equipment with more or different features becomes a part of the competitive strategy of the business.

Stage IV: Leading

In the final stage of progression, leading, the manufacturing organization is looked to as a leader in the development of the competitive strategy of the business. In that role, it is constantly building up its internal resources to apply cutting edge technology to its manufacturing capability. The manufacturing organization is constantly watching the capabilities of the competition to ensure that its organization is as good, if not better. It is a driving force behind the development of the competitive strategy of the business.

Example

Jill is in charge of manufacturing. She is constantly investing in the latest technology and is using it in new creative ways. The business is such that doing what the competition does is not an advantage. New and creative manufacturing processes and procedures must continually be created to stay ahead of the competition. Manufacturing capability is a major force behind the competitive strategy of the business.

COMPETITIVE MANUFACTURING

The broad impact and significance of a new manufacturing system or major capital investment in manufacturing is frequently underestimated. One book refers to the "paradox of capital investment": "It is essential to long-term productivity growth and its impact can be quite powerful. Yet in the short term, depending on the way it is managed, it can reduce total factory productivity and impose substantial costs on the production organization . . . By itself, putting in new equipment will create confusion and make things worse for a number of months" (Hayes, Wheelwright, and Clark 1988).

A major change in a manufacturing system or a large capital investment demands better understanding of the production process. An intimate understanding of the production process is a fundamental source of long-term growth and improvement in efficiency. Therefore, an investment of this nature should be viewed as a step along a strategic path. Investment in capital equipment is a major determinant of how successful a business will be. Since capital equipment defines how a product will be made, it is a commitment to a process. If the process is not the best one, business success will be limited. The cost of undoing a capital investment error can be extremely high. Investing too much, too little, or in the wrong process may never be overcome, especially by a small company. This is, of course, why capital investments are scrutinized so closely by management. If capital investment in general is a critical business commitment, then investment in automated assembly is even more so. Automated assembly equipment is almost always product-specific. Unlike machine tools, packaging equipment, and other more general-purpose equipment, automated assembly equipment has very low resale value. Only a competitor is likely to be able to use it without extensive modification. This makes the risk involved in special purpose automated assembly equipment higher than other, more universal equipment.

Honda is a successful automobile manufacturer because it spends an enormous amount of time understanding the manufacturing process (Main

1990). Typically, a U.S. company puts two-thirds of its effort into developing a product and one-third into developing the manufacturing process. The Japanese companies reverse these two ratios.

Continued capital investment is a key ingredient to a healthy business. "The most profitable time for a company often occurs between the time it stops investing and when it goes out of business" (Hayes, Wheelwright, and Clark 1988).

THE WORKFORCE AND PRODUCTION PHILOSOPHY

Manufacturing's expectations of equipment operators and production people have changed dramatically. It is essential to understand the current expectations of manufacturing when designing new manufacturing systems. For example, machine operators are generally expected to perform quality control inspections on the products in addition to doing much of the routine equipment maintenance and product changeover. In the past, these tasks were assigned to quality control (QC) or maintenance personnel.

The expectations of the workforce change the concept of system design. Since operators are now expected to perform a wider variety of tasks, equipment must be designed to make the operators as efficient as possible. Modern capital equipment projects can:

- Provide machine diagnostic and status displays that supply needed information and are quickly and easily understood;
- Make adjustments easier through the use of scaled indicators or positive stops;
- Include instrumentation to provide feedback so operators can verify the effect of adjustments;
- Be designed so that jams and machine stops can be cleared as quickly and easily as possible;
- Make product changeovers as simple as possible through features such as snap-in-place tooling;
- Involve production representation in early system development.
- Provide thorough operator training that includes safety and electromechanical relationships;
- Design with good ergonomics in mind; and
- Plan for noise avoidance during design.

NEW TECHNOLOGY AND MAINTENANCE CAPABILITY

Many state-of-the-art assembly systems involve technologies that may not be familiar to plant operators or maintenance personnel. If the plant has been through the startup of similar automated systems in the past, adjustment can be relatively easy. On the other hand, if this is the first attempt at automated assembly or if the new system increases assembly speed significantly, change can be a major challenge.

Sometimes the manufacturing plant expresses the desire to obtain equipment that maintenance can handle with current skills and capabilities. This is a dangerous precedent and should be reviewed very carefully. An adequate manufacturing infrastructure is essential for successful automated manufacturing. Highly automated equipment requires skilled, educated operators and maintenance. If the necessary operator and maintenance skills cannot be provided, there are only two options—more downtime or less advanced equipment. Either option results in a less competitive operation. It is incorrect to assume that we can advance manufacturing competitiveness without increasing personnel capabilities. This issue needs to be discussed openly and a compromise reached so that plant personnel feel confident they will be able to learn and manage the necessary skills.

EFFECTIVE PLANT INVOLVEMENT

The success of any project depends greatly on the involvement of the plant's operating and maintenance personnel. Although this involvement is important for any new equipment, it is absolutely essential in the case of automated assembly. The skill, training, and attitude of the operators have a major impact on the efficiency of any new automated assembly equipment and on how quickly it meets expectations. A team effort is key to the success of any automation project, and plant operators and maintenance must be part of the team.

Plant staff involvement should continue throughout the project. Some suggested areas of involvement are:

- Start training during the final phase of debug. This gives plant personnel insight into equipment functions, setup procedures, jam clearing, machine restart, and fault message recognition;
- Get plant personnel involved in decisions concerning system usability (operator panel design and location, fault message descriptions, ergonomic issues, guard design, machine access, and so on);
- Allow the plant personnel to have a voice in any final changes or modifications to the equipment before acceptance;
- Train plant operators to run the equipment before the acceptance run on the shop floor; and
- Involve plant staff in review of the equipment specifications (see Chapter 2 for a suggested list of items to include in equipment specifications).

Select production representation carefully. An operator may not add to general discussions in early stages. Interviewing several operators one-on-one when more specific alternatives can be discussed may be more productive. However, operators can provide valuable input if they are currently producing the product or have some experience with it.

Involvement of plant personnel will help to ensure that they feel comfortable with the required tasks and take ownership of the equipment. If the plant personnel perceive the equipment to be of the quality they desire, they will make every effort to ensure that it meets or exceeds production goals. The same equipment, without plant involvement, can be viewed as something they are forced to live with. They may not take care of it and, in some instances, will not make the effort necessary to meet production goals.

Consider these important questions in predesign meetings with plant staff:

1. Have the acceptance criteria been defined?
2. Have existing/future requirements been considered for:
   - Utilities;
   - Plant production space; and
   - Access (installation, operation, maintenance).
3. Are plant personnel capable of maintaining this equipment with current expertise?
4. Who will provide plant engineering and operator training?
5. How will the following items be considered in design?
   - Preventive maintenance procedures;
   - Automatic or permanent lubrication;
   - Predictive maintenance (self-monitoring/self-diagnostics);
   - Reliability and maintainability of individual components;
   - Maintenance accessibility, guard removal;
   - Ease and frequency of adjustments;
   - Lockout/tagout;
   - Equipment hazard reviews; and
   - Safety.
6. Will ease of alignments and quick changeovers be considered in design?
7. Will special tools or instruments be required to maintain equipment?
8. Are the plant's requirements clearly specified?
9. Is there a preferred component list?
10. Will prototyping be required?
11. Has the acceptable product quality level been defined?

12. Is product quality defined objectively?
13. Does a process flow map exist?
14. Who has previous experience in this type of assembly, internal or external, and is their expertise being used?
15. Are possible short- and long-term changes in the product being considered in the equipment design?

EARLY USE OF SENIOR-LEVEL KNOWLEDGE

As the project progresses, the opportunity for senior-level people to influence the outcome without causing additional delays decreases rapidly, as shown in Figure 1-1. It is important to encourage management and senior technical staff involvement during the early phases of concept and system development. It may seem wise not to confer with management until a project is well developed, but precious time will be lost if management doesn't agree with the direction. It is equally important to involve senior technical people in these early phases to ensure the best technical solutions are considered.

WHAT IS FLEXIBILITY?

Manufacturing frequently requests a "flexible manufacturing system." Although flexible manufacturing is a valid business objective, the definition of this "flexibility" can greatly impact the cost and complexity of a manufacturing system. Flexibility is not free. The tradeoff may be higher equipment cost or reduced efficiency or something else. It is important to balance the tradeoffs to obtain the best utilization of capital investment and production efficiency to support the business objective. Certainly any opportunity to make equipment more flexible should be taken advantage of when the added cost and/or reduced efficiency are minimal. However, since attempts to design in too much flexibility can result in a machine that does nothing well, the tradeoffs must be made clear to all.

When trying to determine how much to automate, the "80/20 rule" is often a good place to start. Rank the products by volume, then automate the highest 80% and provide flexible work cells for the lower 20%. A flexible work cell might consist of fixtures and assembly aids instead of automated equipment. When flexibility is of primary importance and automation is desired, robotics should be considered (see Chapter 5). The most flexible system is a totally manual one. As the manufacturing process develops from manual assembly toward automation, flexibility decreases. That is, as equipment is added, it is added to accomplish a specific task, which in itself begins to limit flexibility. The flexibility to

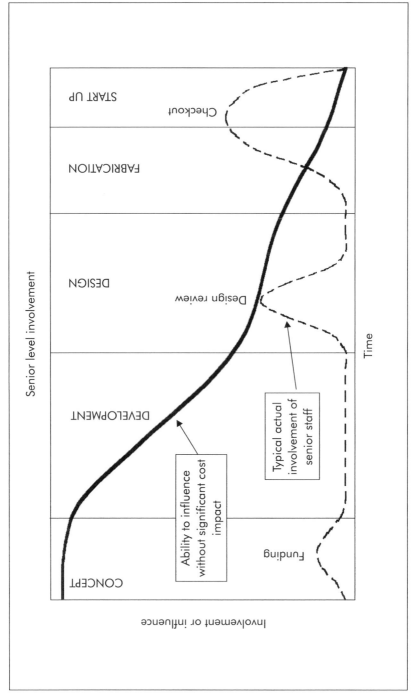

Figure 1-1. Project involvement of senior-level people (adapted from Hayes, Wheelwright, and Clark 1988).

handle additional combinations of the same product family or new, but similar, versions of the same product can usually be accommodated in an automated system. Combining like products is referred to as *group technology*. If product migration/evolution is expected, the desired flexibility must be thoroughly discussed and included in the specifications.

When dealing with questions of flexibility in the arena of high volume products, a discussion on "quick changeover" may be a productive way to address the issues. For example, if the business need is to change from producing one product to a different product quickly or frequently, the effort should concentrate on quick changeover. *Changeover time* is the time elapsed between manufacturing the last acceptable product A and manufacturing the first acceptable product B. A concentrated effort to minimize changeover time can yield remarkable results, frequently reducing changeover from hours to a few minutes.

The number of product variations or stock keeping units (SKUs) actually manufactured on an automated system is often higher than the equipment designer originally anticipated. As products mature and the business grows, so do the number of product variations and therefore the frequency of changeovers. For example, 35 mm photographic film was manufactured by one company in two basic film types (print and slide) with three film speeds for each. Each of these was manufactured in three exposure counts (12, 24, and 36). The number of basic products then was 18 ($2 \times 3 \times 3$). However, because the film was manufactured for a number of private brands, the total number of SKUs was more than 230. Although many of the changeovers were in artwork and packaging, they were still changeovers. Changeover time becomes even more important when the equipment is expected to produce 230 variations compared to 18.

Flexibility is possibly the most elusive manufacturing objective to define and attain. It means different things to different people. It is therefore well worth the time early in a project to define the expectations of manufacturing and laboratory personnel regarding equipment flexibility and future product changes. A good understanding and communication of these expectations can make the final system far more effective and less costly. In the end, the flexibility required of an automated system should be dictated by the business objectives.

SUMMARY

Capital investment is a vital and critical component of the competitive strategy of a manufacturing business. Too much or too little capital investment or investment in ineffective technology will cause a business to lose competitive position. Neither management nor equipment designers can determine the correct technology without a good understanding of both business goals and technical options. They must work together and explore all the options and tradeoffs. Although capital investment is vital to long-term competitiveness, it frequently causes short-term disruption. However, the improvement in process understanding that comes with most major capital projects drives the long-term health of the manufacturing operation.

REFERENCES

Hayes, Robert H., Wheelwright, Steven C., and Clark, Kim B. 1988. *Dynamic Manufacturing*. New York: Free Press: 21-24; 76; 172-172; 279.

Main, Jeremy. "Manufacturing the Right Way." May 21, 1990. *Fortune*: 54.

2

General Principles

CONCURRENT DEVELOPMENT

Most manufacturing system projects can be divided into two parts: prefunding and postfunding, as shown in Figure 2-1. The prefunding phase begins when the product concept or need is first identified and ends when management approves the funding. The postfunding phase is the time until first production or until project goals are met.

Often, a great deal of time and effort is spent on an idea before the equipment engineer is involved in the process. Many decisions are made and the direction set before the equipment engineer is asked to "get it done." The equipment engineer is seen as an implementer. This role does not take advantage of his or her knowledge that could improve the product and manufacturing process.

Concurrent engineering, where all functions are involved in parallel rather than in series, has come to be standard practice in most organizations. However, this important concept is generally applied only to the postfunding period of a project. To maximize the entire product introduction cycle, concurrent engineering should be practiced from the first product concept. Certainly, the equipment engineer is not required full-time, but the input and advice of someone knowledgeable in manufacturing equipment at the earliest stages is necessary to achieve a world-class manufacturing operation. This will require a change in attitude not only by research and development (R and D) but by the equipment engineer who has come to define his or her role as an implementer only.

The reason for not involving certain functions earlier is often that it is not an efficient use of time. This may be true. However, this reasoning sub-optimizes the efficiency of the individual at the expense of the total product introduction cycle. Which is really most important to the organization?

As stated in the introduction, automated assembly equipment tends to be more unique than other types of equipment. Because of this uniqueness, the project cycle may need to be modified. One consideration is early involvement of equipment designers. The more specialized the application, the earlier the equipment designer should be involved.

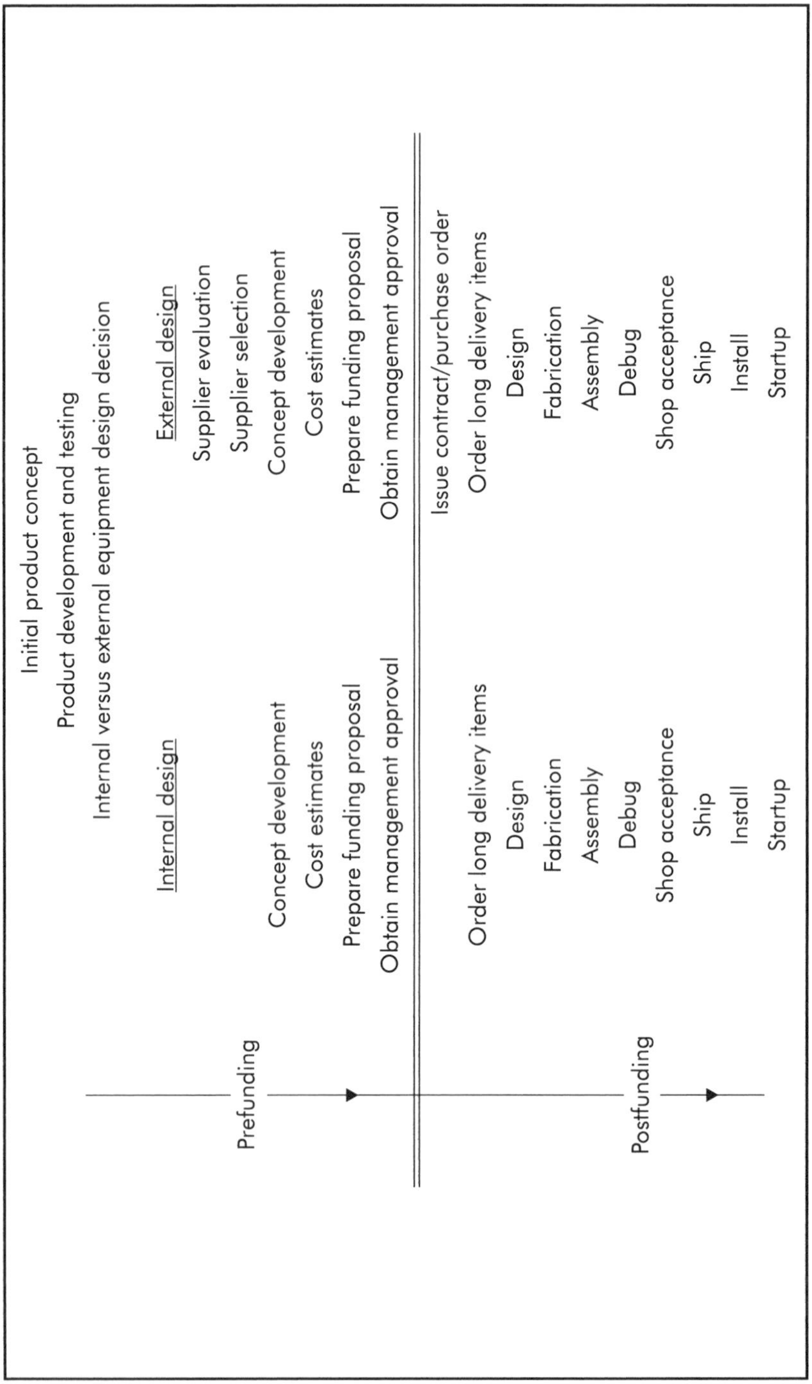

Initial product concept

Product development and testing

Internal versus external equipment design decision

Prefunding →

Internal design

Concept development

Cost estimates

Prepare funding proposal

Obtain management approval

External design

Supplier evaluation

Supplier selection

Concept development

Cost estimates

Prepare funding proposal

Obtain management approval

Postfunding →

Order long delivery items

Design

Fabrication

Assembly

Debug

Shop acceptance

Ship

Install

Startup

Issue contract/purchase order

Order long delivery items

Design

Fabrication

Assembly

Debug

Shop acceptance

Ship

Install

Startup

Figure 2-1. Development cycle for an automated assembly project.

Figure 2-1 shows that a major difference occurs in the project cycle if the design is contracted to an outside supplier. In this situation, it is advisable to select the outside design supplier earlier and involve them in the development process. This requires selection of the supplier based on factors outside the typical bidding process, since specifications are not yet available. The design supplier should become a partner in the project cycle. Obviously, this requires much more of a trust relationship than other buyer/supplier relationships. See "Supplier Evaluation" later in this chapter.

THE TEAM APPROACH

Traditionally, engineers worked primarily alone on a project for several months before presenting their design at a design review. This is not an effective method for today's automated assembly projects because it does not effectively use the body of knowledge available from other sources. Nor does it allow rapid progress early enough to compete at the speed necessary in the present market environment. It is strongly recommended that a team approach be used starting in the early phases of system development, as shown in Figure 2-2.

The team can be an informal group made up of experienced people from a variety of areas related to the particular task at hand. This allows for a very fast start in developing options and can result in substantial progress in a short period of time. The more complex the proposed manufacturing system, the more important and valuable the team approach becomes. The use of a team is important throughout a project but becomes especially critical again during the debug, checkout, and startup phase as discussed further in Chapter 10.

FOCUSED BRAINSTORMING

One of the more effective methods for developing useful solutions is a modified version of the traditional brainstorming technique. This modified version encourages more interaction among team members while avoiding criticism of ideas and unrelated topics. Instead of taking turns offering ideas, members are allowed to build on the ideas of other members. This method can be called *focused brainstorming* since it tends to focus more attention on development of only the best ideas. Solutions, with options, are usually developed during one session, thus providing project direction very quickly.

Focused brainstorming is less disciplined and more difficult to manage than traditional brainstorming. However, once the team members gain experience and feel comfortable with this method, it is more productive,

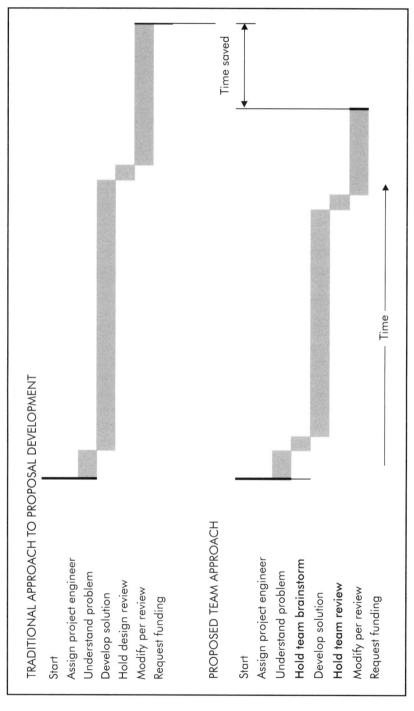

TRADITIONAL APPROACH TO PROPOSAL DEVELOPMENT

Start
Assign project engineer
Understand problem
Develop solution
Hold design review
Modify per review
Request funding

PROPOSED TEAM APPROACH

Start
Assign project engineer
Understand problem
Hold team brainstorm
Develop solution
Hold team review
Modify per review
Request funding

Time saved

Time

Figure 2-2. The team approach.

takes less time, and tends to produce more workable options. It may take several sessions before team members become comfortable with this method. When two or three of the members are comfortable with the technique, they can help lead the process.

Selection of team members is critical to team success, and careful consideration should be given to which disciplines and personnel are represented. People who know how to ask the right questions are often as valuable as those who know the technical answers. Ideas should be listed on poster paper where everyone can see them.

Because accelerated development schedules are becoming a major issue in most programs, focused brainstorming can reduce months off the begining of the product development process and is essential in today's competitive marketplace. As a general reference, a one-month delay in the early engineering phase of a program results in a three-month delay in delivery of the product.

GATHERING SYSTEM INFORMATION

The fastest way to get started on system development is to use a team of people with appropriate experiences. However, project justification must be established before the team meeting. Whether the justification is safety, cost reduction, volume increase, or something else, sufficient information should be presented to satisfy the team that their time is being well spent. Projections of unit cost, market volume, and any related information should be shared. Not only will this information show the participants the project is viable, but it will be critical to many of the recommendations they make. In a short time, a team of experienced people can provide a relatively accurate estimate that can help identify which options to pursue first in the development phase. It is important to stress the "time to decision" at this stage. An estimate accuracy of $\pm 20\%$ is usually more than sufficient to drive the group toward the best options.

When generating concepts for manufacturing, it is always wise to produce alternate proposals and to note the advantages and disadvantages of each option. This minimizes the chance for developing tunnel vision and provides management with some options to evaluate. It also broadens thinking in the development process.

The Delphi technique can be useful in arriving at a "group estimate," as shown in Table 2-1. The premise of the *Delphi technique* is that a series of individual estimates, refined by group feedback, will become less dispersed. The optimum estimate is based on the median response of the group.

Table 2-1. The Delphi Technique

Step 1	Experts create separate estimates.
Step 2	Individual estimates are weighted and combined.
Step 3	The combined, weighted estimate is returned to the experts for discussion.
Step 4	The experts submit new estimates based on the combined data.
Step 5	The procedure is continued until no greater degree of consensus is necessary.

Whether the task is to reach consensus on a cost estimate, machine speed, or run time, the Delphi technique can provide useful information. Although it is time consuming, this technique can be reasonably accurate and is worth using for critical factors. Use it only to get a group estimate of a specific parameter, such as cost, after a specific scenario has been defined.

Highly automated assembly systems are seldom undertaken without some initial manufacturing to provide market samples and startup quantities. The methods, fixtures, or semi-automatic equipment used to provide initial production are a valuable source of information. This initial production equipment should be designed so that information can be gathered to refine the process, as well as provide product.

ASSEMBLY PROJECT PLANNING SOFTWARE

A large percentage of automated assembly projects are never funded. Considerable engineering effort goes into defining, estimating, and developing capital funding proposals for these projects only to find they cannot be justified or are dropped for some other reason. It has been estimated that as much as 30% of an engineering department's time may be spent on projects that are never funded. The efficiency of an engineering department can be improved tremendously if potential projects are evaluated quickly and a go/no-go decision is made before significant engineering time is spent.

A computer-based software application can speed the go/no-go decision on new assembly machines. With minimal input, such as size, component materials, and assembly speed and accuracy, the program provides estimates of equipment cost, time, and resources. The transfer methods that best fit the requirements are listed together with costs and engineering hours by discipline. An estimate of preliminary engineering hours can be provided for the funding proposal. If a proposed project looks justifiable, a more detailed analysis can then be done (Automation Association, Inc.).

DESIGN REVIEWS—GETTING MAXIMUM VALUE

Reviews are frequently viewed as an exercise that should be dispensed with as easily and quickly as possible. The value of a design review is not realized unless experienced people are involved and enough time is allowed to go into as much detail as necessary to uncover potential flaws. A thorough review on a major piece of equipment could easily take a full day or more.

Reviews should begin during the final concept phase and continue periodically until the design is final. At least four reviews are recommended at the stages of concept, design, preship, and preproduction. All disciplines should be involved to ensure that process peculiarities and potential problem areas are fully understood.

There are two primary purposes for design reviews:

1. To ensure the technical soundness of the design; and
2. To ensure that the design meets the user's requirements and specifications.

A design review should include people with the highest level of skill in the technology being reviewed and focus on technical soundness in addition to how well the design solves the business or production problem. Participants in a review should be selected for their knowledge and potential contributions. It is desirable to have everyone involved to aid in communication and "buy in." However, more than eight people is generally too many for a productive technical review. If a large number of people need information, consider giving a "project report" after the technical review. The results of the technical review will add credibility to your plan.

The first (concept) review is the most important. At this stage, confirm that the general approach is correct. Concentrate on the basic business requirements and reasons for your decisions. Often a broad range of backgrounds can be useful in uncovering unique approaches. Brainstorming may be appropriate at an early concept review but is not useful at a later design review.

The objectives of each review should be well laid out and adhered to. It may be helpful to enlist the help of a moderator or facilitator to keep the review on track. If a senior person has been involved as a mentor or advisor, he or she can be a big help in keeping the discussion on important issues.

SAFETY REVIEWS

Conduct safety reviews in the same sequence as design reviews, that is, at each of the four phases of a project (concept, design, preship, and preproduction). If the safety review is scheduled at the end of a design review, it takes relatively little time to complete. By holding the initial safety review early in the design process, safety issues can be avoided completely or resolved with minimal cost. In safety reviews, it is important to concentrate on safety issues as separate from other issues. Include the following questions in any equipment hazard review.

- Flammable liquids:
  - Does the equipment or any anticipated process (including cleaning) require the use of flammable liquids, or combustible liquids heated above their flash point?
  - Is it reasonably expected that flammable liquids will be handled (including cleaning) near or around this piece of equipment?
  - Will equipment be located near flammable liquids or fire hazards?
- Will this machine or any of its anticipated processes (including cleaning) require the use of toxic chemicals?
- Does this equipment contain radiation sources from:
  - Electron beams?
  - Beta gages?
  - X-ray sources?
  - Radioactive materials?
  - Lasers?
  - Ultraviolet light?
  - High-intensity visible or infrared light?
  - Microwaves (ovens)?
  - Intense magnetic fields?
- Does this equipment have any fluid pressure hazards:
  - Pressure vessels greater than 6 in. (15 cm) in diameter (or diagonal) with an anticipated pressure in excess of 15 psi (103 kPa)?
  - High-pressure lines (in excess of 15 psi [103 kPa])?
- Will this machine or any of its components or intended processes generate noise in excess of 80 dB from the following sources:
  - Product noise?
  - Machine actions?
  - Process machinery?

- Plastics production?
- Material handling?
- Use of air?
- Will this piece of equipment or its anticipated processes involve any egonomic issues, such as requiring operators or maintenance workers to:
  - Lift/move objects?
  - Perform repetitive movement operations?
  - Sit or stand in static positions?
- Is overhead material handling required?
- Does the machine have moving parts or high or low temperature hazards?
- Are there any internal forms of potential or kinetic energy that could pose a hazard during operation, cleaning, or maintenance operations?
- If these hazards cannot be eliminated, what warnings and/or labeling, instructions, and/or training are required?

PROCESS VARIABILITY

Process understanding is widely accepted as necessary for proper control of a coating or mixing operation. Yet, the same level of attention is rarely given to an assembly process, even though understanding and control of variability are equally as important. For example, ultrasonic welding must be well defined for the specific application before attempting to incorporate it into an automatic process. The welds must be simulated under conditions that may be seen in production, such as variation in part dimensions, position, variation in fixtures, or variation in air pressure.

Sometimes, a process will behave quite differently when operated at full scale versus a one-up prototype. For example, a ribbon bow product was a difficult packaging problem. Four strands of ribbon needed to be placed neatly into folding cartons. A novel approach was generated and prototyped in a one-up format. The prototype worked beautifully and a 10-up machine was built. Unfortunately, the 10-up format created so much static electricity that the bows would not stay in the package.

The progression of process understanding is shown in Table 2-2. Reactive and preventive control focus on resolving problems with existing processes. Progressive and dynamic control move upstream in development to avoid control problems and, in the case of dynamic control, ensure control of new processes.

Table 2-2. Progression of Process Understanding

Level	Knowledge	Skills	Who
Reactive	Tell good product from bad	Identify bad product, develop solutions to abnormal variations	Production operator
Preventive	Identify sources of abnormal variation	Attention to detail, discipline, and procedures to eliminate abnormal variations	Production operator with process engineering support
Progressive	Describe existing processes in quantitative terms	Analysis and process development to identify normal variations	Partnership between product, process, and equipment engineers—creative engineering
Dynamic	Understand principles governing proposed processes	Research, experiment, integrate science and engineering, define the optimum process	Product, process, and equipment engineering teams, advanced engineering departments, highly skilled engineers and scientists

(Adapted from Hayes 1988)

PROCESS WINDOW

The *process window* can be defined as the range of process conditions that result in acceptable product. Successfully incorporating a process step into an assembly system requires careful definition of the process window using designed experiments. These techniques can be learned from courses that are available, or request the help of someone skilled in this area. As a minimum, be familiar with the basics and application of designed experiments in defining the process window.

UNDERSTANDING INCOMING MATERIALS & COMPONENTS

In the past, the efficiency of an automated assembly operation, whether good or bad, was attributed almost entirely to the equipment itself. Today, those experienced in automated assembly equipment generally agree that 50% of all automation problems are due to input materials and parts. Whether or not one agrees with this estimate, it is a fact that material quality, variability, and defect level have a direct and profound impact on the efficiency of an assembly machine. *No matter how good an assembly operation is, it can be made better by improving the consistency of input materials.* To achieve the most competitive manufacturing operation, all elements of the assembly system must be optimized. It has been said that "an automatic assembly machine is a 100% inspection device; it finds every bad part we put into it and stops." An understanding of component variability is essential to achieving high levels of equipment efficiency.

The quality level of components provided by suppliers for manual or low-speed assembly is often inadequate for higher speed assembly. Statistical sampling methods may be sufficient for three-sigma quality levels but become inadequate when the target is six-sigma. So called "qualified suppliers" are often qualified using statistical sampling methods that are not adequate for high-speed manufacturing.

Early in an automation project, the definition of a defect may not be the same for the plant as it is for the design engineer. Quality data reported by production personnel is usually aimed at identifying variations that cause a functional or appearance problem in the product. Plant personnel are often less aware of dimensional variations that cause problems in automated assembly. The most common example of this is a product that is currently assembled manually. It is unlikely that the plant has an accurate measure of component variability or defect level. This is because the manual assembly operator adjusts for component variations, thereby masking assembly problems that will surface during automated assembly. This is why *the first venture from manual assembly into automated assembly is the most difficult.*

One definition of quality is described as "defect-free performance in all products and services provided to the customer" and continues, "For a company aiming to design products with the lowest possible number of defects, traditional three-sigma designs are completely inadequate" (Smith 1993).

Component Characteristics

Startup problems are almost certain to occur if product drawings are assumed to be truly representative of product components "Actual production parts may vary widely from part prints or written specifications if these specifications do not reflect actual production capabilities or functional requirements of the product" (Riley 1983). Since part prints are rarely based on actual process or production capability, they cannot be trusted. Figure 2-3 shows several actual examples of the distribution of part dimensions compared with drawing specifications. It is extremely important to evaluate product components for critical assembly dimensions before beginning the design phase of an automation project.

Initially, engineering has to take the lead in determining part quality level and, if required, how it can be improved to facilitate the assembly process. Product, process, production, and supplier personnel all need to participate in this effort. Although assembly equipment should be designed to be as forgiving as possible, a coordinated effort to reduce component defects results in lower overall manufacturing costs.

In addition to a careful evaluation of the initial components, attention must be given to any component changes during the life of the project. For example, a change in component material can result in unexpected process changes. Never assume that a material change does not affect the process, even if it is the first impression. As molds and tools wear, changes occur. Flash on molded parts may increase and burr on cut edges may increase. Consider material stiffness and strength if the part is put under a load in the process. More subtle differences also can have an effect. Colorant in a molded part or ink color on a printed paper part can change the way a part feeds, transfers, or interacts with a mating part. In one example, paperboard cards printed with red ink had a different surface lubricity than cards printed with other colors. This caused the cards to feed differently, and made it necessary to adjust the machine for a color change.

In another case, a change from one plastic material to another (part dimensions within the same range) caused machine output to change from nearly 100% good parts to 0% good parts. Careful realignment of the tooling at a transfer point improved the situation, but another tooling component had to be redesigned using a lower friction material. The

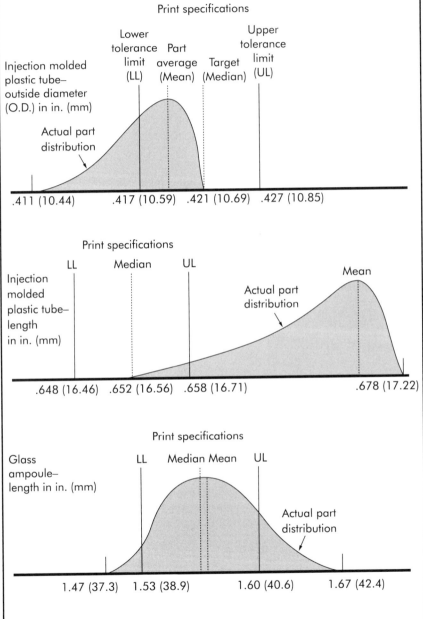

Figure 2-3. Actual part dimensions compared with print specifications.

reason for the problem? The new material was slightly softer than the old and, more importantly, had a higher coefficient of friction surface. The molding process and material combined to give the original part some surface lubricity that the second part did not have. This caused the new parts to be misaligned in one half of the tooling and then damaged as the other half closed on the part.

In a third example, a molder changed from using 10% regrind to 100% virgin resin to mold a part. The resulting parts met all specifications yet would not run in the automated assembly machine. Investigation determined that the 10% regrind "deadened" the part while the 100% virgin parts were so resilient they bounced and became misaligned.

Watch for the following variations in component parts:

- Dimensions;
- Surface finish;
- Moisture content (paperboard, plastics, etc.);
- Lubricants or lack of (paperboard, plastics, etc.);
- Burr (some processes cause a burr that varies depending on tool wear);
- "Clean and dry" (means different things to different people);
- Direction of grain (most sheet and roll materials have a "grain" and perform differently down web versus cross web);
- Color changes (colorants and inks can affect properties); and
- Static electricity (especially important when handling lightweight parts).

EVALUATING PART VARIABILITY

If actual production parts are available, even if they are not the final design, make these determinations early in the project:

1. Part versus print dimensions. Determine which dimensions are critical to automated assembly.
2. Dimensional variability. Measure a few parts (at least one from each cavity or tool) to verify that the dimensions match the print or, more typically, to identify which dimensions don't match.
3. Defect level. Measure at least one significant dimension of a quantity of parts (10 to 30) to determine what normal variability can be expected. If this initial check shows a potential concern, measure more parts. (Machine vision inspection is an excellent way to make repetitive inspections, especially on deformable parts. Machine vision systems collect data automatically and display the results in a useful format with no additional effort. Large quantities of parts can be inspected quickly using a vision-aided robot to feed the parts.)

4. Estimate the number of defective parts (short shots, flash, mouse bites, etc.) that can normally be expected. If reliable production data is not available, estimate the defect level based on similar processes for which historical data is available. Defect levels are typically expressed in parts per million (ppm). If a process is well controlled, a defect level of 40 ppm or less should be attainable. If the defect level is not tracked and controlled, it will be higher (200 to several thousand ppm). As assembly speed increases, defect level has an increasing impact on run time. Likewise, the more components in the product, the more impact defect level has on run time. Examine the amount of dirt or other foreign material included with the components. Equipment often can be designed to minimize the amount of debris that actually gets into the product.

Table 2-3 lists typical defect levels for high-volume metal, injection-molded plastic, and paper component parts. The information is categorized according to typical defect level ranges for average and well-controlled manufacturing processes. Typical defect levels are listed as a ppm range to account for varying degrees of component manufacturing difficulty and a number of other variables that go into determining manufacturing quality level. Counts listed include functional and visual (cosmetic) defects and indicate the level of defective components shipped from the component manufacturer to the product assembly plant. The information was culled from various component manufacturers, production plants using these components, and technical experts from the respective fields. Since few component manufacturers inspect 100% of their product, production plants using the components in an assembly are the best source of defect level data. Although production plants don't generally inspect 100% either, defective components are often caught at assembly or during quality audits performed at the plant. Unfortunately, jams at the assembly machine are often the main source of feedback that component parts are defective.

Defect Levels in Metal Parts

The defect levels for various metal manufacturing processes are listed in Table 2-3 from least difficult to most difficult, with forming being the toughest process to control. Most metal components undergo multiple processing steps. Therefore, the appropriate defect level is the one corresponding to the most difficult process step in manufacturing the component.

Defect Levels in Plastic Parts

The defect levels for injection-molded plastic components are listed in Table 2-3 as a function of the type of component specifications that must be met. As indicated, the addition of tight visual specifications can drastically increase the defect level. Injection-molded plastic data assumes multiple cavity molds since components assembled into high-volume products are usually produced from multiple cavity molds. Theoretically, a single cavity mold produces fewer defective components, but would not meet component volume requirements.

There is no size-related affect on defect levels in the small-to-medium size range of component parts generally used in high-volume assemblies. This is because of current improvements in mold design and control of the injection molding process. Defect levels generally increase when dealing with micro-sized or large components that have tight specifications. Large components are defined as larger than 6-8 in. (15-20 cm) in two major dimensions.

Table 2-3. Defect Level of Components by Manufacturing Process

Component/Manufacturing Process	Defect Level (defects per million parts)	
	Average Process	Well–controlled Process
Metal		
Punching size	100-1,000	0-100
Punching location	100-1,000	0-100
Stamping	150-1,500	0-150
Forming	200-2,000	0-200
Injection-molded plastic (multiple cavity)		
Tight dimensional specifications only	200-1,000	0-200
Tight dimensional and visual specifications	1,000-5,000	0-1,000
Paper		
Die-cut paperboard:		
Assembly components		
Virgin board-SBS*	200-1,000	0-200
Recycled board	500-1,500	0-500
Packaging components		
Virgin board-SBS*	1,000-5,000	0-1,500
Recycled board	2,000-10,000	0-3,000
Die–cut label:		
Size	10-50	0-10
Registration	50-250	0-50
*Solid bleach sulfate		

Defect Levels in Paper Parts

Defect levels for die-cut paperboard and die-cut labels are listed in Table 2-3. Paperboard is the semi-rigid, .010-.028-in. (0.25-0.71-mm) thick paper product typically used for hanger cards, backcards, or for folding cartons in packaging. While paperboard components in assemblies are generally simple and flat, those used in packaging are generally more complex and involve various score lines and gluing. Due to differences in manufacturing complexity and respective defect levels, assembly and packaging paperboard components are listed separately in Table 2-3. Defect levels for paperboard components are also broken down into virgin solid bleach sulfate (SBS) and recycled board categories. Although the environmentally sound and popular course in the 90s has been to use recycled paperboard where possible, bear in mind that the inconsistencies associated with recycled paperboard can often double the component defect level. Generally, greater process capability must be designed into equipment to handle recycled paperboard components. The defect levels listed in Table 2-3 assume that laser rule dies are used to manufacture the paperboard components. Hand-cut rule dies should be avoided and could significantly increase the defect level.

It is unwise to delay investigation of component part variability until after the equipment is built because the level of component defects has a major influence on the uptime of high-speed automated assembly or packaging equipment. The economic impact of high component defect levels and subsequent low machine uptimes can be drastic. Initiate efforts to measure part variability and ensure that defect levels are within targets as soon as parts are available for evaluation. The goal is to design critical tooling using part dimensional information gathered during the part variability evaluation. Improving quality and minimizing defect level is an ongoing process. However, do not postpone the tasks until the assembly or packaging equipment hits the plant floor.

Defects Caused by Shipping

Never overlook the need to take great care in the shipping of delicate component parts. Much painstaking work is wasted if they are damaged during shipping.

Initial Part Evaluation Procedure

Before starting the design phase, request specific part samples for evaluation. Do not accept parts of unknown origin or process conditions for this purpose. Parts must be typical of regular production-run samples and not hand-selected parts. Keep records of all available part information, including date of run, lot number, process conditions, and other pertinent data.

Molded Parts

Evaluate three molded parts from each cavity from three different runs. The best way is to have the runs made from resin lots with melt indexes at the top, middle, and bottom of the acceptable range. A color change should be considered a different part until color is shown to have no effect on dimensions or properties.

Evaluation of All Parts

Evaluate 30 parts from each of three lots.

1. On at least one sample of each part, measure all dimensions that are critical to the assembly process.
2. Produce a histogram and sigma distribution graph of the measurements. Most machine vision systems have this capability built in.
3. Determine the process variability for each dimension, and make sure the design concept can tolerate the part limits that the process variability indicates.
4. Evaluate the current part process for possible changes to improve part quality and to facilitate the assembly process.

Part Variability of Manufacturing Processes

If production parts are not available, estimate the likely variability of the components. Use the best data available and solicit the advice of people familiar with the processes used to make the components. The variability of some common processes is shown in Table 2-4. Note that many factors, such as material and tool wear, also affect variability.

Estimating the variability and defect level early in the project allows further investigation of potential problems at the proper time rather than during checkout or startup. Both component quality (component manufacturing process) and the assembly concept must be optimized to obtain maximum system efficiency. The idea that the assembly machine should be designed to accept wide variations in incoming components dooms the manufacturing operation to subpar performance. *Automated assembly should be addressed as a system, and all parts of that system should be optimized to achieve maximum system efficiency.*

The best process is when parts not meeting specifications do not reach the automated assembly machine. Parts should be pre-inspected and all defective parts discarded. However, because pre-inspection is not always done or not always 100% effective, anticipate defective parts reaching the assembly machine. Design the machine so that defective parts or assemblies pass through without stopping or jamming. This is one of the most important concepts in high-speed assembly, and is discussed in more detail in Chapters 3 and 9.

Table 2-4. Variability of Components by Manufacturing Process

Manufacturing Process	Notes	Variability in. (mm)		
		Common Practice	Closely Controlled	Precision
Metal stamping				
Blanking contour	Linear dimensions	±.015 (±0.38)	±.007 (±0.18)	±.003 (±0.08)[1]
Hole location	Depends on die design	±.005 (±0.13)	±.003 (±0.08)	±.001 (±0.025)
Formed bend location	Depends on die design and material uniformity	±.010 (±0.25)	±.005 (±0.13)	
Formed bend location	Depends on die design and material uniformity, as well as thickness, hardness, grain, and radius size (smaller radius is more consistent)	±1°	±1/2°	
Multispindle high-production screw machine[2]				
Length of part	Depends on location of features such as grooves, shoulders, etc.	±.005 (±0.13)	±.003 (±0.08)	±.001 (0.025)
Diameter		±.003 (±0.08)	±.001 (±0.025)	±.0005 (±0.013)

[1] Fine blanking and shaving: ±.001 (±0.025).
[2] Data based on conventional six-spindle automatic screw machine. Assumes machine is in good condition with tools kept sharp.

Table 2-4. Variability of Components by Manufacturing Process (continued)

Manufacturing Process	Notes	Variability in. (mm)		
		Common Practice	Closely Controlled	Precision
Injection molded plastic[3]				
Greater than 1 in. (25.4 mm)	Same cavity	±.005 to ±.020 (±0.13 to ±0.5)	±.0004 to ±.005 (±0.01 to ±0.13)	
Greater than 1 in. (25.4 mm)	Multicavity	±.007 to ±.020 (±0.18 to ±0.5)	±.0005 to ±.002 (±0.013 to ±0.05)	
Less than 1 in. (25.4 mm)	Multicavity	±.003 to ±.010 (±0.08 to ±0.25)	±.0002 to ±.002 (±0.005 to ±0.05)	
Rule die cutting[4]				
Laser-cut die		±.003 to ±.030 (±0.08 to ±0.76)		
Hand-cut die		±.020 to ±.06 (±0.56 to ±1.5)		
Die-cut paperboard	Laser-cut die	±.005 to ±.015 (± 0.13 to ± 0.34)		

[3] Injection molded part accuracy by mold design, mold quality, type of plastic, molding machine controls, and settings. (Shrinkage rates for injection molded plastics vary from .001 to .040 in. per in.)
[4] Part consistency is dependent upon accuracy of die.

Table 2-4. Variability of Components by Manufacturing Process (continued)

Manufacturing Process	Notes	Variability in. (mm)		
		Common Practice	Closely Controlled	Precision
Die-cut paperboard	Hand-cut die	±.020 to ±.040 (±0.05 to ±1)		
Die-cut label registration (with preprinted artwork)	Laser-cut die	±.015 to ±.020 (±0.38 to ±0.5)		
Die-cut label registration (with preprinted artwork)	Hand-cut die	±.015 to ±.030 (±0.38 to ±0.76)		
Die-cut label size	Laser-cut die	±.010 to ±.015 (±0.25 to ±0.34)		
Die-cut label size	Hand-cut die	±.015 to ±.030 (±0.34 to ±0.76)		

Table 2-4. Variability of Components by Manufacturing Process (continued)

Manufacturing Process	Notes	Variability in. (mm)		
		Common Practice	Closely Controlled	Precision
Die casting[5]				
Zinc	For a 1 in. (25.4 mm) length	±.010 (±0.25)		±.002 (±0.05)
	For each additional in. (25.4 mm)	±.001 (±0.025)		±.001 (±0.025)
Aluminum	For a 1 in. (25.4 mm) length	±.010 (±0.25)		±.002 (±0.05)
	For each additional in. (25.4 mm)	±.001 (±0.025)		±.001 (±0.025)
Copper	For a 1 in. (25.4 mm) length	±.014 (±0.35)		±.007 (±0.18)
	For each additional in. (25.4 mm)	±.003 (±0.076)		±.002 (±0.05)

[5] Part consistency is dependent upon tooling design, quality, and material.

When to Inspect

One option for detemining and maintaining quality is the use of online inspection to detect major flaws expected in incoming parts. Defective parts can be removed immediately or the remaining operations can be "locked out." Such on-line inspection of incoming parts may sound like overkill, but in fact, it can result in significant improvement in reliability. In some cases, pre-inspection of parts may be warranted. The part supplier may be able to provide inspection at minimal cost.

It is usually more desirable to inspect parts at the time they are manufactured so that problems can be corrected quickly. However, many things can happen to introduce defects in a part between the time of its manufacture and its arrival at the assembly operation. Winter cold, summer heat, and large differences in humidity can all affect the stability of components, in addition to the physical stresses caused by transportation and handling. For example, paperboard is notorious for handling differently depending on the humidity. Paperboard and other hygroscopic materials may have variability associated with humidity changes from summer to winter. Extreme temperatures can cause variability such as warping of plastic parts shipped in summer. Precision fits or measurements require controlled temperature at assembly. Make the when-to-inspect decision based on actual production experience, if possible.

PROTOTYPING

Assembly systems are rarely so straightforward that production machine design can begin without some experimentation or prototyping. There are two levels of prototyping:

1. Proof-of-concept prototyping; and
2. Proof-of-process prototyping.

Proof-of-concept Prototyping

The first level of prototyping is called proof-of-concept prototyping, and is usually a very simple and expeditious approach. Its purpose is to determine if the basic concept will work. Avoid the temptation to spend a great deal of time designing and analyzing at this point.

The fastest route to learning what will work is to try a few things. Start by checking the parts or process—how do they feel? do they slide on one another? do they interlock?—and then start doing experiments using simple fixtures. Progress toward a proof-of-concept prototype in steps. In this way, whether you have successes or failures, you will be learning and moving toward a solution with little time or cost invested. The objective is to keep the cost of any failure low and quickly build knowledge of what will and will not work. It is worth trying some unlikely but posssible options at this stage—you may be pleasantly surprised. Proof-of-concept prototypes are usually not intended to run more than a few hundred parts and will not provide a quantitative measure of process reliability, only an intuitive judgment.

Prototyping is an important learning process and the lessons learned must be carried into the design. The easiest way to ensure this is to have the same people involved in both prototyping and equipment design.

Proof-of-process Prototyping

Once the concept is proven feasible by a proof-of-concept prototype, a more elaborate proof-of-process prototype may be warranted. This depends on the difficulty and risk of the operation and any questions that remain unanswered. The usual objective of a proof-of-process prototype is to determine the reliability or robustness of a process step. Process verification often requires running large quantities of parts through numerous cycles using extensive instrumentation. Use statistical analysis to determine the run size for the confidence level desired.

Be sure the objectives and resource costs are clear before starting. Proof-of-process prototypes can be expensive, but they can also provide valuable information. The level of reliability needed for any operation depends on project objectives for run speed, uptime, and quality. Define acceptable reliability before building the prototype to determine the number of cycles for which to plan. The impact of reliability requirements is discussed further in Chapter 3.

SIMULATION

Computer modeling and simulation are powerful tools that can augment physical prototyping. Designs can be analyzed and improved before any metal is cut. Motions can be observed and refined using animation. These useful tools need to be part of any automated assembly design project. However, a balance must be maintained between computer modeling and actual prototyping. This is particularly true of assembly systems because of the variables involved in handling discrete parts. Less experienced engineers sometimes try to solve too much on the computer when a few experiments would provide better information. Older designers don't always recognize the value of the newest analysis tools. A good understanding and appreciation of each is necessary to decide when analysis is warranted and when it is time to test the idea with a real-world prototype.

SUPPLIER EVALUATION

Selecting the supplier of an automated system is more critical than selecting a supplier for other types of equipment. The success of an automated system depends largely on the skill, knowledge, and expertise that the supplier brings to the project. This is especially true if the supplier will design as well as build the equipment.

Base evaluations of potential suppliers on the skills, experience, and capabilities determined to be important for the particular task at hand. Satisfactory performance on one assembly project does not guarantee that a supplier will perform well on another project requiring a different set of skills. For example, expertise with an intermittent, in-line assembly project may not transfer well to a project involving metal stamping or tape-roll handling. If there has been turnover in the supplier's staff, or if key individuals are not available to work on a project, performance can be very different from project to project. Table 2-5 shows an example of a supplier evaluation. Evaluation is best done by a multidisciplinary team during on-site visits to the supplier. The supplier is not selected based only on getting the best score. There are too many unqualified factors to make this critical decision based on numerical tabulation alone. The evaluation is a good way to organize the discussion of many important factors. There is seldom a clear winner in such an evaluation, but the final choice can be made with in-depth knowledge of the suppliers' strengths and weaknesses. To assure success, the purchaser and supplier should have all the key skills needed between them and work as a team on the project. Although factors such as cost and delivery may seem to be the critical factors during the selection process, technical ability and the ability to perform are actually the most important. If the supplier cannot provide the equipment contracted for, the buyer loses the ability to manufacture and sell product. This is far more devastating to a business than added equipment cost or even late delivery.

Thoughts on cost and quality involving the selection of suppliers are as appropriate today as they were in the 1800s. One such quote: "It's unwise to pay too much, but it's unwise to pay too little too. When you pay too much, you lose a little money—that is all. When you pay too little, you sometimes lose everything . . . because the thing you bought was incapable of doing the thing it was bought to do. The common law of business balance prohibits paying a little and getting a lot—it can't be done. If you deal with the lowest bidder, it is well to add something for the risk you run, and if you do that you will have enough to pay for

Table 2-5. Supplier Evaluation

ABC Assembly Machine: Supplier Evaluation								
Supplier:	A	B	C	D	E	F	G	Weighting
Location	2	1	3	5	5	4	3	1
Welding	1	5	3	5	4	2	1	1
EDM	1	5	5	5	5	5	5	1
Grinding	1	5	5	4	3	2	1	1
CNC	3	1	5	4	2	5	1	1
Inspection	5	1	3	3	5	2	1	1
Wiring	1	1	1	5	2	2	1	3
UL approval	5	5	5	5	5	1	5	3
Assembly facilities	1	4	2	5	5	3	1	3
Status reporting	2	1	2	5	5	2	5	3
Inside versus outside work	1	5	2	5	4	5	2	3
Project management	3	2	1	5	5	5	3	5
Technical staff—mechanical	3	4	5	5	5	4	3	5
Technical staff—electrical	4	3	3	5	5	5	4	5
Applicable expertise	5	2	1	3	3	5	4	5
Previous performance	5	5	1	2	2	2	1	5
Quality of work	3	2	1	5	5	2	4	5
Our confidence	4	3	1	5	5	2	3	5
On-time record	3	2	4	5	5	3	2	5
Schedule, time available	1	5	5	1	1	5	5	4
Predicted cost factor	2	2	5	4	1	3	5	3
Financial capability	2	2	5	2	2	2	1	4
Documentation	5	1	1	5	5	5	5	2
Weighted totals	221	217	202	310	287	246	223	
Weighted rating	5	6	7	1	2	3	4	
Request quote				Yes	Yes	Yes		
Rate each factor from 1 to 5 with 5 being high. Assign weighting to each factor if desired.								

something better" (Rushkin 1905). From the wisdom of the past, we can get a broader perspective and recognize that today's problems are often merely extensions of past problems. Then, we quickly realize that the solutions for today's problems lie in ageless principles.

It is possible to reduce costs on every project, but an equipment engineers' primary obligation is to provide an end product that will do everything it was bought to do.

SUPPLIER SELECTION

The selection of a supplier for an automated assembly project should never be made using cost as the only criterion unless a thorough prebid supplier evaluation has determined that all bidders are equally qualified. It is easy for an inexperienced engineer to acquire a sense of false security believing that good specifications and a strong contract will make a supplier responsible for performance within the agreed upon cost, regardless of what problems are encountered. If the supplier is financially equal to or larger than the purchaser, this may work. However, experience has shown that, when the purchaser is much larger than the supplier, the purchaser usually pays part of any cost overrun—even if the overrun is primarily the fault of the supplier.

The importance of working closely with the supplier of automated equipment cannot be overemphasized. Because of the interaction between the product and components and the assembly system, close communication among all functions is essential. Turnkey automated assembly machines provided by suppliers who are not intimately linked to the purchasers internal functions seldom meet expectations.

Avoid being intimidated by a supplier who says something like "I'll do it your way, but it's your responsibility if it doesn't work." The project or design engineer already has that responsibility. So, if you are sure you are right, don't be afraid to specify how you want it done. Usually, a thorough discussion will clarify the assumptions and eliminate any disagreement. Of course, this discussion should take place before the contract is awarded. Both the purchaser and the supplier should be comfortable with the approach taken. Suppliers tend to specialize in certain types of equipment and have experience with assembling certain types of products. It is usually an advantage to partner with a supplier who has experience with similar products. However, recognize that your competitors probably have access to the same supplier unless an exclusive agreement can be negotiated.

In one study, Powell Niland stated "Because of its distinctive characteristics, the acquisition of special automatic equipment calls for different policies and procedures from those for conventional equipment" (Riley 1983). The study found the following:

- The major difficulty is in developing special automatic equipment;
- The relationship between the designers of special automatic equipment and the product design function is critical, and communication between these functions is essential;
- Careful, detailed pre-award planning is necessary;
- Systematic testing and recording of data should be used during debug; and
- Statistical process control (SPC) techniques are valuable during debug to identify the causes of poor performance.

Although it is necessary to carefully specify the acceptance criteria in the specifications/purchase agreement, this is seldom a straightforward task. On one hand, suppliers frequently inflate their bid when the acceptance criteria are loosely defined. On the other hand, product components that meet specifications in the required quantities are frequently not available. Suppliers know this and, together with the pressures to get the equipment shipped, it gives them a good bargaining position during the checkout and acceptance period.

Estimate the cost (and availability) of the components needed to debug and accept the equipment before completing the acceptance criteria. This cost is frequently significant and often impacts the length of the supplier's debug and acceptance period. A good general reference is to provide three times the number of parts needed for the actual acceptance runs specified. Parts for checkout and acceptance should be high quality, virgin production parts. Do not use scrap parts for checkout or acceptance. Parts can be affected by frequent reuse during checkout, so virgin parts should be introduced frequently. During refeeding, the parts may become polished by handling and actually feed better, giving a false impression of how well the system can run virgin parts.

EQUIPMENT SPECIFICATIONS AND OUTLINE

Automation projects must be driven by the purchaser's engineer. The purchaser's engineer should review scheduled milestones against actual progress and resolve problems and potential delays before they impact the project. The document most important to a successful outcome is the equipment specification. The specification is the foundation on which the project is built.

A sound specification ties the project engineer, plant, and supplier to one document. This ensures that there are no surprises for any of the parties involved. The specification ensures that the supplier understands, in detail, what is expected from the quotation process through installation. Likewise, the plant understands what they have agreed to.

The following outline shows basic items which must be part of an equipment specification.

1. Definition of purpose—use of assembly project planning software for this task is advisable. Define the objective of the project by answering the following questions.
   - What equipment is being provided and why?
   - What is the driving force?
   - Who is the primary driver?
   - What other functions are involved?
   - What are the project constraints?
   - How many operators will be designated to run the equipment?

2. Equipment description—describe the equipment in general overall terms by answering the following questions.
   - Is the equipment one assembly machine or a system comprised of material handling, assembly, and packaging machines?
   - Is the transfer process intermittent, continuous, power-and-free, or other?
   - Does the equipment include piece-part feeders, buffering devices, laser printers, or other special processes?

3. Product specifications—describe the finished product the equipment will assemble by answering the following questions.
   - What is the purpose of the product?
   - What component parts make up the product?

   Include a product assembly drawing and bill of materials (latest revision) in the specification.

4. Piece-part specifications—for each piece part, identify the following:
   - The material the part is made from;
   - The drawing number or specification number with latest revision;
   - Describe any changes that the parts are undergoing or may undergo; and
   - How will the parts be supplied to the machine (bulk, magazine, reel, other, pre-oriented or nonoriented)?

5. Equipment output rates—for each piece of equipment, specify:
   - Design rate;
   - Production rate; and
   - How long the equipment should run without refurbishment.

If multiple pieces of equipment are required, specify rates for each piece. Normally, the design rate should be 20 to 25% faster than the production rate. This provides a safety factor so that the machine does not run routinely at maximum possible speed; it also allows the plant to speed up the equipment for short periods of time to compensate for deficiencies. Production rate is the speed the equipment must normally run at to meet production requirements. More information on estimating production rates is in Chapter 3.

6. Output efficiency—compute and specify efficiency required to meet the forecasted production goals for the life of the equipment. Specify efficiency as a production goal based on percentage of good parts produced and equipment uptime. Make sure that the plant understands and agrees with this figure. This process is described in detail in Chapter 3.

7. Equipment description and sequence of operations—describe, in sequential order, each component of the assembly line, and how it functions and operates. Start with the machine description. For example, a machine that is single-tooled, continuous motion, axis horizontal, in-line with line-shaft driven stations:

- Specify the running height of fixtures above the floor line;
- Designate the approximate length and width of the machine;
- Stipulate the number of fixtures required;
- Cite fixture pitch;
- Show line speed; and
- Describe how each fixture is to function, how it holds and orients the piece parts.

Next, describe each station on the assembly line in detail. For example:

- Station #01—auto feed, orient and place part A onto fixture, inspect for presence and position;
- Part A will be hopper supplied, feeder bowl oriented and fed down an in-line track to a star wheel escapement;
- Parts will be oriented flat side down and nose leading;
- Parts will be separated by the star wheel escapement and transitioned to the placement head;
- A rotary head will be used to pick off parts from the escapement and place them onto the fixture;
- Parts will be placed on the fixture flat side up and nose leading;
- Station will detect part placement and position; and
- List system and station detects so that the plant knows what will be provided and the supplier knows what is required.

The listing should include a description of the condition to be detected, the sensor type, and the required machine reaction to the detected condition, as shown in Table 2-6.

8. Facility requirements—specify the utilities available at the plant production site and list restrictions that could affect equipment design:

- Electrical: ____volts ____ phase____ hertz;
- Pneumatic: ____ pounds per square inch-gage (PSIG) Maximum. Is air clean and/or dry?;
- Vacuum: ____ inches of mercury (Hg);
- Ceiling height;
- Floor loading;
- Ventilation;
- Lighting;
- Door openings;
- Dock height; and
- Floor space availability (make sure this space includes room for equipment control panels that tend to occupy a large amount of space).

9. Safety requirements—itemize safety features required by the plant:

- Noise;
- Guarding;
- Guard interlocks;
- Overload protection;
- "E" stop locations;
- "E" stop operation;
- Manual or jog operations;
- Operator restrictions; and
- Lockout/tagout.

10. Interface requirements—specify mechanical, electrical, and programming interfaces.

11. Equipment construction guidelines:

- Specify the life expectancy of the equipment;
- Specify whether the machine base should be equipped with shock absorbing leveling pads or mounted to the floor using anchor bolts and leveling jacks;
- Specify whether wear parts should be hardened or hard-plated;
- Specify if all mechanical parts not made from stainless steel should be surface treated (painted or plated) to prevent rust;

Table 2-6. Sensor Data

Description	Type	Reaction
Description of system detects		
Low air pressure	Air switch	Machine stop
Line shaft overload	Proximity switch	Machine stop
Transfer conveyor overload	Proximity switch	Machine stop
Guard interrupt	Proximity switch	"E" stop
Description of station detects		
Bowl low level	Proximity switch	Operator warning
In-line track low level	Photo eye	Operator warning
In-line track empty	Photo eye	Cycle stop
Star wheel phase fault	Proximity switch	Machine stop
Placement head phase fault	Proximity switch	Machine stop
Part not on placement head after pick	Photo eye	Machine stop after three consecutive detects
Part on placement head after place	Photo eye	Machine stop
Part not positioned on fixture	Photo eye	Machine stop after three consecutive detects

- List plant equipment paint specifications;
- Specify any preventive measures required for dust, dirt or debris; and
- List equipment lubrication specifications.

12. Control system requirements—specify the equipment's control system. Describe the following items as required:

- Programmable logic controller/personal computer (PLC/PC);
- Data reporting;
- Diagnostic equipment;
- Fault annunciation;
- Drive requirements;
- Motor specifications;
- Operator panel description;
- Control panel description;
- Wiring and wireway requirements;
- Isolation transformers;
- Power supplies;
- Convenience outlets; and
- Underwriters Laboratory (UL) requirements.

13. Training, testing, and acceptance—training of designated personnel should occur at the supplier's facility during the final phase of debug.

Testing requirements—dry run at design speed:

- Dry run time = 24 hours;
- Check equipment every eight hours; and
- Fix or replace defective items; restart test.

Acceptance requirements—equipment run duration (in hours):

- Equipment cycle speed (cycles per minute); and
- Equipment output rate (counting machine-induced defects only).

Equipment efficiency—counting machine-induced stops only:

- Input components not to specification will not count against equipment output and efficiency;
- Specify acceptance requirements at supplier's facility and at final location; and
- Acceptance run at supplier's facility to be performed by purchaser's production operators if possible.

14. Installation requirements include:

- Teardown and crate instructions;
- Method of shipment;

- Insurance requirements; and
- Installation requirements (should supplier provide installation or will purchaser/plant be responsible?).

15. Documentation requirements include:
    - Drawing ownership (computer-aided design [CAD files]);
    - Drawing standards;
    - Spare parts list;
    - Equipment manuals—operation (to include station timing charts);
    - Maintenance;
    - Troubleshooting; and
    - Quantity of manuals required.

    Note: Spare parts list and manuals to be issued before acceptance and CAD files must be updated and in owner's possession before final payment.

16. Quotation requirements—specify how the quotation is to be formatted. Often, it is pertinent to have potential equipment suppliers list engineering labor, shop labor, and purchased components separately for purposes of comparison.

17. Input/output (I/O) list—develop an equipment electrical input/ output list for each process station and for total machine control. This is critical for machine control agreement and quotation comparison.

18. Equipment Schedule—develop a Gantt chart schedule for equipment. Scheduled tasks should include:
    - Mechanical engineering design;
    - Electrical engineering design;
    - Review dates;
    - Fabrication;
    - Assembly;
    - Plumbing and wiring;
    - Debug;
    - Acceptance;
    - Teardown;
    - Ship time;
    - Installation;
    - Start up;
    - Production start;
    - Piece part requirement dates and quantities;
    - Project benchmarks;

- Preferred components list from the plant; and
- Safety standards to be followed.

Note: Computer planning software can provide a projected duration from issue of purchase order through installation. The Gantt chart provided by the equipment supplier should have each station listed separately. This will allow close tracking of progress.

SUMMARY

Automated assembly projects are best handled by a cross-functional team that becomes involved early in the product design to ensure product manufacturability. Regular reviews during a project are important to obtain the opinion of experienced technical people and to confirm that the proposed system will meet production and business goals. Brainstorming techniques can be effective in developing unique ideas and are especially useful early in a project. Requiring alternative proposals is a good way to encourage creative thinking.

Variability is detrimental to an assembly process. Defects and variability in the components to be assembled should be understood very early in an automated assembly project. Although assembly equipment must accommodate some variability, reducing defects and variability will improve total system efficiency as well as product quality.

New, unproven assembly techniques can provide a competitive advantage but can also introduce risk. Simulation and prototyping can be used to manage the risk associated with a new approach. Automated assembly equipment is generally designed for a specific product and process. Although some capital equipment (such as packaging equipment) often can be a modification of a previous design, automated assembly equipment is usually unique and, therefore, requires a more skilled supplier or design team. If a supplier is used, technical capability should be the most important selection criterion.

REFERENCES

Automation Association, Inc., PathQuest™, 3564 Rolling View Drive, Suite D, White Bear Lake, Minnesota 55110.

Hayes, Robert H., Wheelwright, Steven C., and Clark, Kim B. 1988. *Dynamic Manufacturing*. New York: Free Press: 224-225.

Riley, Frank J. 1983. *Assembly Automation: A Management Handbook*. New York: Industrial Press: 17, 45.

Ruskin, John. *Complete Works of John Ruskin*. New York: Crowell, 1905.

Smith, Bill. 1993. *Machine Design:* 64.

Defining the Assembly Process

REVIEW BUSINESS NEEDS AND OBJECTIVES

Determining the best assembly process or transfer method for a given application must start with an understanding of business needs and objectives. Two basic factors need to be considered:

1. Understand where the manufacturing function is within the business and where it is headed. This is discussed in Chapter 1. For example, does the business expect its manufacturing capability to be a major part of its competitive strategy, or is manufacturing just supposed to build the product without any discussion?
2. Understand the production requirement. What is the annual sales forecast and will it be achieved with one, two, or three shifts? In addition to this basic target, related considerations are discussed in this section.

Production Rate Requirements

Based on the annual production need, the first step is to determine what machine rate is required in units per minute using the desired number of shifts and an estimated overall system efficiency. At this point, be careful to be realistic about overall system efficiency. Actual overall system efficiencies are generally much lower than the projected numbers requested. Figure 3-1 provides a quick reference to production requirements. Marketing forecasts, especially for new products, are generally unreliable and can be overly optimistic. Unfortunately, they are generally also the only estimates available. Rather than depend on a single market forecast, request high and low forecasts from marketing. Looking at the equipment needs of high and low scenarios may totally change the perspective on the best approach to meeting business objectives.

After machine rate is determined, you can begin to consider the options. For example, would it be better to use one high-speed line or several slower lines to meet the yearly production requirements? Committing global production to one machine might be cost effective, but it could pose an unacceptable business risk. Using two or three machines might be a better compromise of risk and unit cost.

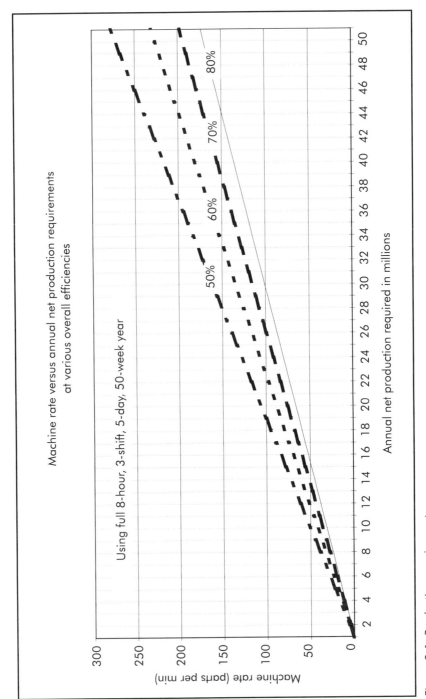

Figure 3-1. Production requirements.

Available floor space is a constraint in many plants. Efficient use of floor space should always be a design goal. Adequate access for operators and maintenance, and space for incoming and finished product are important to operational efficiency and must be considered as part of the space occupied. Working with production staff early in the process will avoid unpleasant surprises.

Maximum machine speed is usually dictated by product design and/ or the assembly process. Review and discuss limitations to assembly speed early in concept development. If limitations due to product or process design are not challenged at this time, the entire manufacturing system will be designed around them, and any chance of making revolutionary product design and process improvements will be lost.

It is equally important to look into creative ways to assemble a product at higher rates without making product or process changes. It is critical to call upon all available expertise at this stage. When the correct expertise is joined together in a functional brainstorming session, as described in Chapter 2, revolutionary ideas for improving product design and processes can be generated within as little as 3 hours.

The objective is to arrive at the best combination of product design, assembly process, and equipment design. Whether this is called concurrent engineering, cross-functional development, or just common sense, all functions (lab, manufacturing, and engineering) must work as a team to arrive at the most effective overall system.

PRODUCTIVITY

Productivity and efficiency measurements are the source of much confusion and misunderstanding. A generally accepted definition of overall equipment effectiveness (OEE) is shown by equations 3-1, 3-2, 3-3, and 3-4 (adapted from Nakajima 1988).

$$OEE = M_a \times P \times Q_R \qquad (3\text{-}1)$$
$$M_a = (\Sigma T - S_{dt} - U_{dt}) \div (\Sigma T - S_{dt}) \qquad (3\text{-}2)$$

where:

M_a = Machine availability—the time that the equipment produced product divided by the time that the equipment was scheduled to produce product.

P = Performance—the time it should take to produce a quantity of output divided by the time it actually took to produce the quantity of output.

Q_R = Quality rate—quantity of acceptable parts produced divided by quantity of total parts produced.

ΣT = Total available time—gross time in period being measured. For example, 480 minutes per shift, 1440 minutes per day (three shifts).

S_{dt} = Scheduled downtime—time equipment is scheduled not to operate. For example, planned maintenance, lunches and breaks, meetings, lack of market need.

U_{dt} = Unscheduled downtime—time equipment is scheduled to operate but is out of service, for example, machine failure, clean up, changeover, set up and adjustment, wait for material.

$$P = [(1 \div M_R) \times O_a] \div (\Sigma T - S_{dt} - U_{dt}) \qquad (3\text{-}3)$$

where:

M_R = Machine rate—speed of equipment determined by process variables, measured in units per time, for example, feet per minute, gallons per hour, parts per minute.

O_a = Output—actual number of units produced during period being measured.

ΣT = Total available time—gross time in period being measured.

S_{dt} = Scheduled downtime—time equipment is scheduled not to operate.

U_{dt} = Unscheduled downtime—time equipment is scheduled to operate but is out of service.

$$Q_R = (O_a - R) \div O_a \qquad (3\text{-}4)$$

where:

R = Rejects—number of units produced during time period being measured that are outside product release control limits. For example, scrap and rework.

Note: Units of time, such as minutes and hours, must be consistent throughout all calculations.

A world-class operation is where:

Availability = $>.90$
Performance efficiency = $>.95$
Quality rate = $>.99$

The overall equipment effectiveness then is:

$$.90 \times .95 \times .99 \times 100 \cong .85 \qquad (3\text{-}5)$$

An OEE of .85 is a good target, but as we will see later in this section, it is a difficult target and, depending on the complexity of the operation, may take considerable time and effort to reach. OEE should not be a stand-alone measure. For example, increasing the speed of an event-based operation like assembly will probably decrease OEE, but still may be the right business decision. OEE is a relative measurement useful in tracking continuous improvement in one process. It should not be used as an absolute measurement to compare different processes.

To optimize the productivity of an automatic line, use a finer division of causes than that offered by OEE. Figure 3-2 provides a more detailed description of the factors impacting net system output. Since most of these factors are affected by several different job functions (production operators, production management, maintenance, engineering, and design), look at enough detail so that the key players can act as a team to address each opportunity.

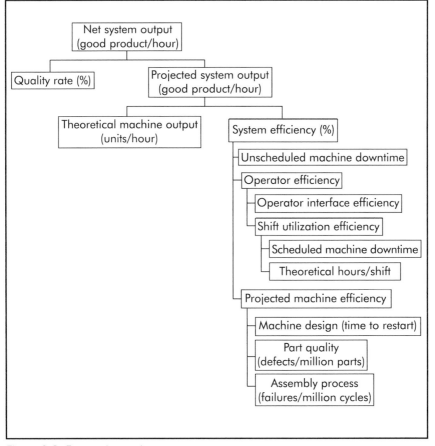

Figure 3-2. Factors impacting net system output.

Even where responsibility rests primarily with one function, factors are often influenced by other functions, as shown in Figure 3-3. The startup of new systems—especially systems new to a plant—will be much smoother if all functions participate in discussing the contribution each makes to the overall operation. A manufacturing system will never reach its full potential unless all functions understand their impact and work toward system optimization.

Example

An assembly system requires a plastic part supplied by another company. Purchasing can negotiate the best price by purchasing in larger quantities. The supplier would mold a 6-month supply and stock the balance to be delivered as needed. However, the longer the parts are stored, the more they are deformed by their own weight and the weight of the parts on top of them. After 6 months, the parts will have a much higher defect rate and create more jams and defective product. This will probably end up costing more in lost production than is saved by a bulk purchase agreement.

Components, such as packaging supplies and plastic parts, often have a shelf life that determines how long they can be stored and still used efficiently in automated assembly equipment. For example, paperboard scores self-heal over time and plastic parts have internal stresses that deform the part over time. Heat and humidity can accelerate these actions. The most efficient manufacturing system is one where all factors are optimized for the total system rather than for each factor individually (suboptimization).

RUN TIME/DOWNTIME

Much discussion centers on the subject of run time, but little is based on fact. Run times of 80% to 90% or more are frequently requested by manufacturing, and engineering often has little or no basis for questioning the requests. Even after the run time for a new system is agreed upon, little analysis is done to ensure that it can be reached.

Example

A finely tuned mature assembly operation produced a product consisting of 15 plastic and metal components. Five years after installation, system run time had increased to an average of 83%, based on a 7-day, 4-shift schedule. With the implementation of a sophisticated predictive maintenance program, run times increased to 88% and nonconforming product decreased by 51% in the first year. During this period, there were continuing improvements in equipment design.

Factor	Engineering/design	Production management	Maintenance	Operators	Process engineering	Product support/warehouse and stocking/purchasing	Suppliers	Lab/mktg
Theoretical machine output (machine rate)	X							
System efficiency								
1. Unscheduled machine downtime	X		X			X	X	
(Wait for material, product changeover/setup, cleanup, maintenance knowledge, maintenance response, machine failure)								
2. Operator efficiency								
Operator interface efficiency		X		X				
(Machine loading, operator knowledge, operator response, reporting/recording, quality inspection)								
Shift utilization efficiency								
Scheduled machine downtime		X	X	X	X			
(Lunch breaks, process experiments, planned maintenance, meetings, lack of demand)								
Theoretical hours/shift		X						
(Crew scheduling)								
3. Projected machine efficiency								
Machine design	X							
(Time to restart, operator interface, ease of changeover, ease of maintenance, susceptability to jamming)								
Part quality		X			X	X	X	X
(Defects/million, design for assembly, handling/storage damage, aging damage)								
Assembly process	X				X			X
(Product design, assembly method, packaging design)								
Total	4	4	2	2	3	2	2	2

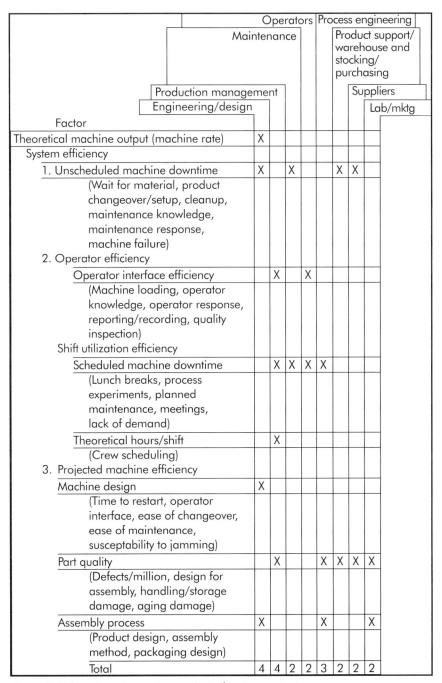

Figure 3-3. Functions impacting projected system output.

This example indicates that it takes significant time and financial investment to achieve 80% to 90% run times.

Using standard design and maintenance procedures, run times much greater than 80% are difficult to achieve. In a production setting, many issues other than equipment speed and complexity contribute significantly to downtime. Incorporating predictive maintenance procedures, reducing or automating changeovers, and eliminating stops for meetings or lunch breaks can substantially increase run time.

Insufficient data is available to determine a "typical" downtime profile, but Figures 3-4, 3-5, and 3-6 show the breakdown of production time for three actual production lines. The following sections explore some techniques for improving run times.

Time to Restart—Minimizing and Avoiding Downtime

Four elements control the net output of a manufacturing system:

1. The machine as a system.
2. The reliability of the individual station functions.
3. The motivation of the operating and maintenance personnel.
4. The uniformity of component parts supplied to the machine.

The most effective way to increase uptime is to reduce the time to restart (Riley 1983). Although the average time to restart is heavily dependent on operator motivation, the machine design engineer can have a great impact as well. It also should be noted that operator motivation is very dependent on how frequently a machine jams and how difficult it is to clear. Since jams are inevitable, one way to reduce restart time is to design the machine so that jams can be cleared quickly without damaging the machine. Use of quarter-turn screws, snap-in-place tracks, hinged doors, and spring-loaded covers are examples of quick-access design. Some examples of quick-clearing designs are shown in Chapter 9. As mentioned earlier, adequate access and ease of access are also important considerations during design.

Another option for the design engineer is to design feed tracks so that the parts can be easily seen by the operator who can then clear any problem before a machine stop occurs. The best solution, of course, is to "recognize" defective parts before they cause a jam and either automatically reject them or pass them through the machine without adding value. Although passing a defective part through the machine causes a loss of one unit of output, it is far better than stopping the machine in most cases. In one high-speed assembly line, it was determined that a defect that caused a stop resulted in lost production of 38 units, while passing the defective part through caused a loss of only one unit. In any

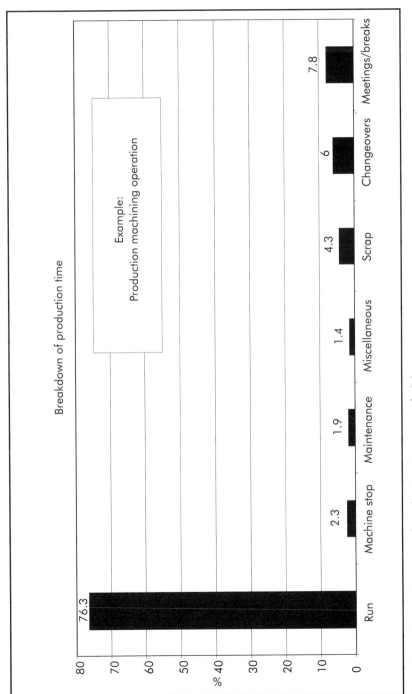

Figure 3-4. Typical allocation of production time, example (a).

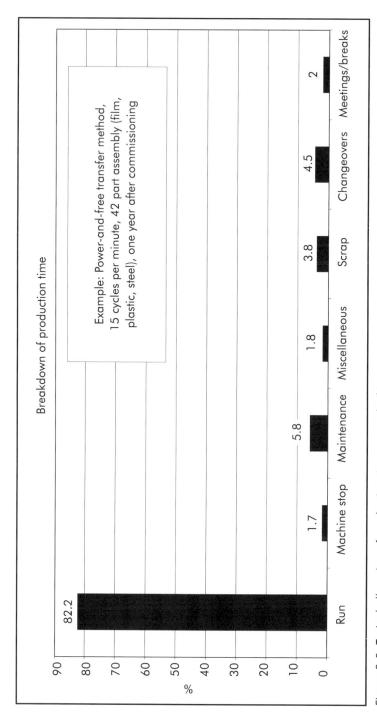

Figure 3-5. *Typical allocation of production time, example (b).*

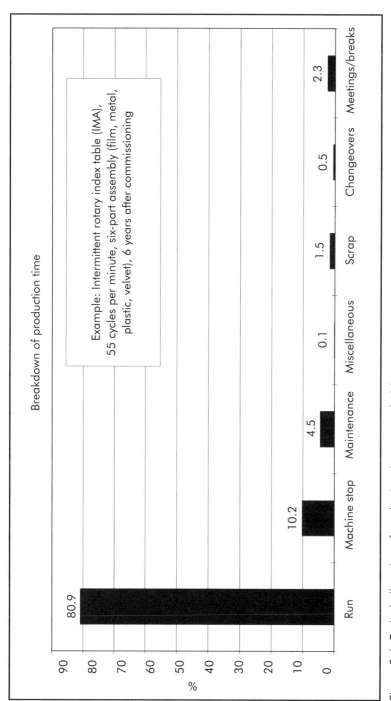

Figure 3-6. Typical allocation of production time, example (c).

case, care must be taken never to allow defective parts or product to be mixed with the good output and ultimately be passed on to the customer.

Run time and Reliability

High-machine run time is one of the primary goals in modern automated assembly systems. Yet, there appears to be very little understanding of the factors influencing run time. This section examines the factors affecting the reliability of an assembly system and details some of the ideas mentioned in earlier sections.

For purposes of this discussion, we are concerned only with defects that cause a jam. Therefore, the term *defect* as used here means "jam-causing defect." In practice, only some flawed parts cause a jam. Flawed parts that do not cause a jam must be detected by inspection or testing and rejected, or they will end up in products to be sold. Percent of machine downtime is determined by equation 3-6.

$$U_{dt} \ (\%) \ = \ [U_{dt}/(U_{dt} + R_t)] \times 100 \qquad (3\text{-}6)$$

where:

U_{dt} = Unscheduled machine downtime—this is the time a machine should produce product but doesn't.

R_t = Run time—the time during which a machine should make a product and does.

Total time is downtime plus run time.

Causes of Downtime

While run time is quite straightforward, downtime has different causes. Factors included in downtime calculation vary from plant to plant. All machine- and part-induced stops are generally included, but change-overs or machine cleanup may or may not be. Changeovers and cleanup are often included in scheduled machine downtime (see Figure 3-2). Before discussing downtime, reach a clear understanding of what is included and what is not.

Unscheduled machine downtime always includes the following:

- Machine breakdowns (bearing failure, motor failure);
- Process failure (bad placement, bad fastening process); and
- Component failure (defective component, such as a broken or incomplete part).

In most assembly operations, process failure and component failure are far more significant than machine breakdown.

Because component failure can be related to defects in incoming components, the effect of component defects on machine downtime will be discussed in detail. This does not mean that process failure is less important. In fact, it may be the more important of the two. However, process failure is more specific to the particular assembly process and more difficult to analyze because process failure rates are difficult to obtain. Process failure is usually addressed by prototyping and testing as described in Chapter 2. Analyzing the effect of process failure on downtime can be done using the technique explained next, and can be very useful in uncovering potential problems while changes can still be made before system design is complete.

The percentage of downtime attributed to defective components that cause jams is:

$$D_t\,(\%) = \frac{R}{R + [1 \div M \times P \times (d \div 10^6)]} \times 100 \qquad (3\text{-}7)$$

where:

D_t = Downtime (%).
R = Average time to restart (minutes per jam).
M = Machine speed (units per minute).
P = Number of parts per unit.
d = Defects (defective parts per million parts) or jams (jams per million parts).

The variable d assumes every defective part causes a jam. The term *unit* refers to a complete product assembly. The terms *part* and *component* are used interchangeably and refer to the individual pieces that make up a unit. For example, to demonstrate the effect of variables on downtime calculation, assume the following.

M = 50 units per minute
P = 5 parts
$P \times M$ = 50 units per minute $\times$ 5 parts = 250 parts consumed per minute

First, look at the effect of defective parts on the assembly operation. If we assume the parts are 99.95% good (5 parts in 10,000 cause a jam), then 250 $\times$ 5/10,000 = .125 or one part jams every eight minutes on average. If the average time to restart (R) is two minutes, then $D_t = 2/(2 + 8) = 20\%$ downtime for part jams alone.

Although 99.95% good parts may seem reasonable at first, it is not good enough for an efficient assembly operation. The impact of reducing defects can be seen in Table 3-1. Note that the reliability of process operations, such as ultrasonic welding, impact run time in a similar manner. Although these factors have a big impact at 50 parts per minute, the impact is even greater as machine speed increases. Tables 3-2 and 3-3 show the effect of increasing machine speed M, assuming an average part defect level (d) of 500 and 40 parts per million (ppm), respectively.

Very high-speed assembly operations generally involve two or three components and very low defect levels (less than 10 ppm). On-line inspect/reject for each component can be used to minimize stops caused

Table 3-1. Results of Reducing Defect Level (d) on Downtime (D₁)

Machine speed (units per minute)	M	50	50	50	50
Number of parts	P	5	5	5	5
Parts consumed (parts per minute)	PM	250	250	250	250
Average time to restart (minutes)	R	2	2	2	2
Defects (parts per million defective)	d	40	100	250	500
Downtime (%)	D_t	2.0%	4.8%	11.1%	20.0%

Table 3-2. Results of Increasing Machine Speed (M) on Downtime (D₁) with d = 500

Machine speed (units per minute)	M	50	100	200	500
Number of parts	P	5	5	5	5
Parts consumed (parts per minute)	PM	250	500	1000	2500
Average time to restart (minutes)	R	2	2	2	2
Defects (parts per million defective)	d	500	500	500	500
Downtime (%)	D_t	20.0%	33.3%	50.0%	71.4%

Table 3-3. Results of Increasing Machine Speed (M) on Downtime (D₁) with d = 40

Machine speed (units per minute)	M	50	100	200	500
Number of parts	P	5	5	5	5
Parts consumed (parts per minute)	PM	250	500	1000	2500
Average time to restart (minutes)	R	2	2	2	2
Defects (parts per million defective)	d	40	40	40	40
Downtime (%)	D_t	2.0%	3.8%	7.4%	16.7%

by defects and effectively reduce the defects actually seen by the assembly operation to 10 ppm or less.

Time to Restart

As stated earlier, time to restart is the single most important variable affecting production rates. Tables 3-4, 3-5, and 3-6 show the impact of reducing average time to restart (R) for three different combinations of machine speed (M) and defect level (d).

The reliability of each assembly process and transfer is equally important in achieving an efficient machine. Consider the number of processes and part transfers: each has a failure rate and, if no buffer is provided, they are additive. Once the impact of each element is understood the importance of doing a reliability analysis early in the design process is apparent.

Table 3-4. Results of Reducing Time to Restart (R) on Downtime (D_t) with Machine Speed $(M) = 50$ and Defect Level $(d) = 500$

Machine speed (units per minute)	M	50	50	50	50
Number of parts	P	5	5	5	5
Parts consumed (parts per minute)	PM	250	250	250	250
Average time to restart (minutes)	R	0.5	1.0	1.5	2.0
Defects (parts per million defective)	d	500	500	500	500
Downtime (%)	D_t	5.9%	11.1%	15.8%	20.0%

Table 3-5. Results of Reducing Time to Restart (R) on Downtime (D_t) with Machine Speed $(M) = 50$ and Defect Level $(d) = 40$

Machine speed (units per minute)	M	50	50	50	50
Number of parts	P	5	5	5	5
Parts consumed (parts per minute)	PM	250	250	250	250
Average time to restart (minutes)	R	0.5	1.0	1.5	2.0
Defects (parts per million defective)	d	40	40	40	40
Downtime (%)	D_t	0.5%	1.0%	1.5%	2.0%

Table 3-6. Results of Reducing Time to Restart (R) on Downtime (D_t)
with Machine Speed (M) = 500 and Defect Level (d) = 40

Machine speed (units per minute)	M	500	500	500	500
Number of parts	P	5	5	5	5
Parts consumed (parts per minute)	PM	2500	2500	2500	2500
Average time to restart (minutes)	R	0.5	1.0	1.5	2.0
Defects (parts per million defective)	d	40	40	40	40
Downtime (%)	D_t	4.8%	9.1%	13.0%	16.7%

In summary, the variables that determine machine run time are:
- Machine speed;
- Reliability;
  - Based on the number of parts/operations;
  - Of each part/operation; and
- Time to restart.

A reasonable estimate of machine performance can be determined by estimating variables and calculating different scenarios.

Operators can get fatigued and slow down if they have to clear jams more frequently than every 5 minutes on average. This usually equates to about 60% run time. If this level of reliability or higher is not expected, a lower speed, at least initially, may yield better results as well as more cooperative operators.

SEPARATE VERSUS COMBINED OPERATIONS

The goal of reducing cycle time in manufacturing encourages the integration of operations. Ultimately, the fastest cycle time from raw material to finished goods is obtained by linking all process steps together in one manufacturing line. Although a totally integrated line is "the ultimate" streamlined solution, it can be a disaster if the reliability and interaction of each operation is not well understood.

Successfully integrated processes, such as bottling lines, have evolved over many years of progressively moving closer and closer to full integration. Integration of less proven processes needs to be done carefully and is usually accomplished gradually with careful planning. The primary concern when integrating operations is the reliability of the individual operations, since this is what determines how many operations can be linked together while still maintaining a reasonable run time.

Buffers or accumulators are used between the integrated sections of a manufacturing line to minimize the effect of individual section downtime on the total line. Buffers in high-volume assembly present a circular problem. Buffers increase the overall efficiency of a line. However, in high-volume operations, a few minutes' supply of parts can take up a great amount of space, so parts are often stored in bulk form as buffers. Feeders are then necessary to reintroduce the parts to the next operation, but are often the least reliable components in the entire assembly line, greatly contributing to downtime. Hence, the circular problem. The size and location of buffers deserves very careful investigation because it can have a major impact on the run time of the total line. Computer simulation is very useful and strongly recommended to help make this determination.

With the preceding cautions in mind, the advantages of integrating operations can be very significant. As just-in-time (JIT) manufacturing has shown, the lack of in-process inventory forces recognition of process shortcomings. This rapid feedback greatly improves process understanding and can help to improve the operation.

Injection molding, stamping, box forming, and packaging are examples of operations that should be considered for on-line integration. Performing these operations on-line eliminates handling of in-process materials to and from the warehouse, reduces waste, and improves quality.

JIT manufacturing is not a new concept. The following is Henry Ford's vision of manufacturing for the Ford Model T (Hayes 1988):

> "Our system consists of planning the methods of doing the work as well as actually doing the work . . . Our aim is always to arrange the material and machinery and to simplify the operation so that practically no orders are necessary . . . Our finished inventory is all in transit . . . Our production cycle is about 81 hours from the mine to the finished machine in the freight car, or 3 days and 9 hours instead of 14 days, which we used to think was record-breaking . . . Let us say one of our ore boats docks at Fordson at 8 o'clock on Monday . . . minutes after the boat is docked, its cargo will be moving toward the high line and become part of the charge in the blast furnace. By noon Tuesday, the ore has been reduced to iron, mixed with other iron in the foundry cupolas, and cast. Thereupon follow 58 operations that are performed in 55 minutes. By 3 o'clock in the afternoon, the motor has been finished and tested and started off in a freight car to a branch for assembly into a finished car. Say it reaches the branch plant so that it may be put into the assembly line at 8 o'clock Wednesday morning. By noon, the car will be on the road in the possession of its owner."

One strategy for achieving integrated manufacturing while minimizing risk and lost production is to move toward full integration in phases, as shown in Figure 3-7. Over a period of time, the system slowly becomes very efficient.

Example

A case history of integrating a process from molding through final packaging on a product consisting of 33 components produced the following results:

- 14% Daily unit output increase;
- 15% Material cost reduction;
- 30% Unit cost reduction;
- 31% Space reduction;
- 42% Nonconforming product reduction;
- 60% Labor hours reduction;
- 80% Material handling and transportation cost reduction; and
- 98% Manufacturing cycle time reduction.

These gains were over a 3-year period that included ongoing equipment improvements. However, in most cases, over half of each individual gain was achieved within the first year after the completed integration. This project is a good example of a well-implemented, totally integrated system. However, there is one significant caution: it is not possible to achieve these results on a project of this magnitude without a cooperative team effort. An experienced leader is needed in each discipline: controls engineering, design engineering, maintenance, management, manufacturing, and project engineering. Without an experienced leader in each area, items can be overlooked and cause significant problems at the implementation phase. The duration of this project, from initial design through startup, was approximately 4 years. As noted earlier, total integration happens over a period of time.

In this project, packaging was automated first and tied into the output of the assembly process. The most challenging aspect for engineering was the design effort required to integrate molding with assembly. The control and process problems involved in accumulation and deaccumulation from many different presses with different cycle times feeding into several assembly lines can be overwhelming. To achieve the results described on a complex system like this with as many product components involved, six-sigma quality levels coming off the presses have to be the norm.

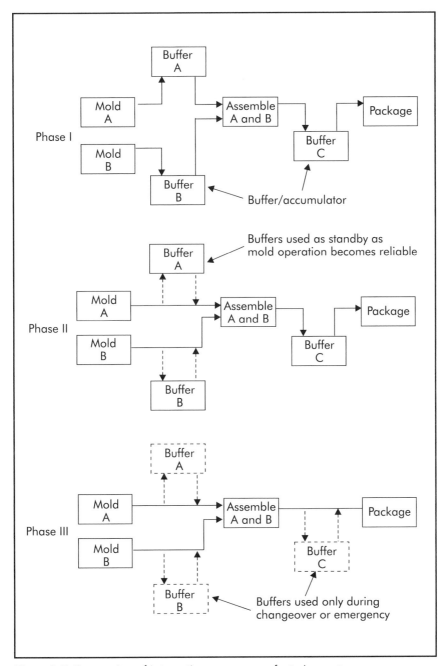

Figure 3-7. Progression of integrating a new manufacturing system.

ACCUMULATION (BUFFERS)

Properly located and designed buffers are essential to achieving high run time on complex manufacturing lines. Location and sizing can be best determined using computer simulation. The design of buffers is critical, since they easily can be the cause of downtime rather than the cure. Buffers must be reliable to be effective.

An example of the impact of buffers on efficiency is shown in Figure 3-8. *Efficiency* is defined as the number of acceptable products a system actually produces in a given time divided by the theoretical rate it should produce. This example assumes a station efficiency of 95%, where 4% of lost efficiency can be recovered by adding buffers after each station, and a nonrecoverable loss of 1% remains. The efficiency after adding a buffer to each of the four stations is 92% as compared to 81.5% without buffers.

Buffers can be designed for last in, first out (LIFO), first in, first out (FIFO) or random operation. LIFO and random buffers are usually simpler. Unfortunately, most manufacturing operations require FIFO designs to maintain production control. Examples of buffer designs are shown in Figure 3-9. Figure 3-10 shows the output sequence resulting from a combination FIFO/LIFO buffer (Figure 3-9e) with four parts per stack.

CONSTRAINTS SUCH AS SIZE, SHAPE, AND RIGIDITY

The products addressed in this book generally fit inside a 6-in. (15-cm) cube. Larger product is often difficult to handle at assembly rates above 60 ppm. One exception is web products, such as 8.5 × 11-in. (22 × 28-cm) sheets.

Component shape can be a limiting factor if storage and handling become cumbersome. Frequently, high-volume products involve one or more components that have little rigidity. Handling soft parts, which are common in disposable products, can be one of the most challenging problems in automated assembly. Soft components require different techniques than those used for rigid metal or plastic components. Other component material characteristics, such as weight/density and brittleness, also should be considered.

The most common technique for handling soft components during assembly is to keep them in web form until they are placed in the product or assembly fixture (a *web* is a continuous thin, flat material that will become a component or acts as a carrier for a component). If this is not possible, the individual parts are sometimes reattached to a carrier material until final placement. Some methods of assembling soft parts are shown in Figure 3-11.

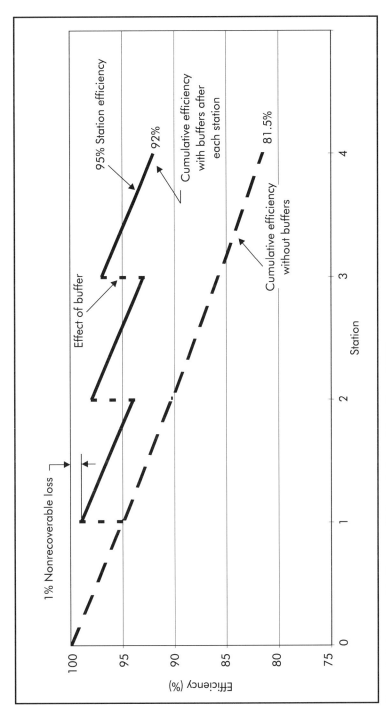

Figure 3-8. Impact of buffers on efficiency (adapted from Treer 1979).

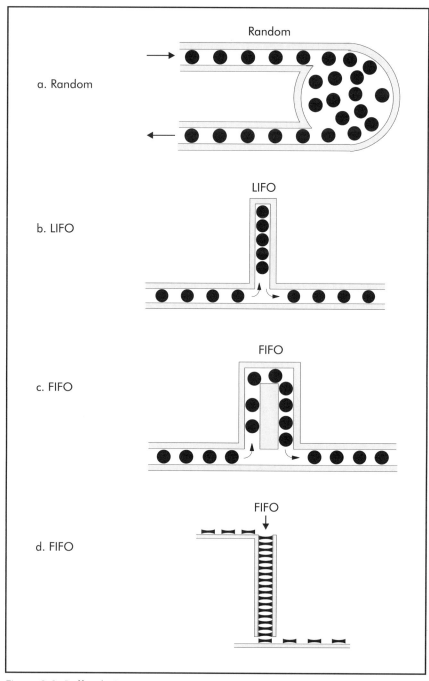

Figure 3-9. Buffer designs.

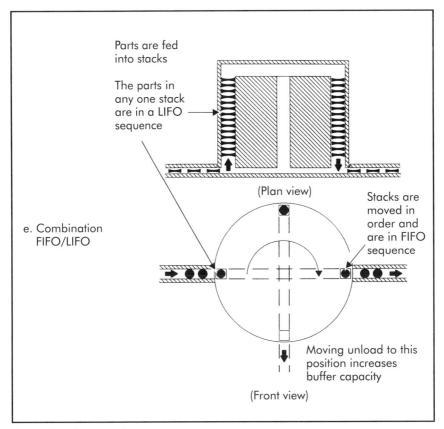

Parts are fed into stacks

The parts in any one stack are in a LIFO sequence

(Plan view)

e. Combination FIFO/LIFO

Stacks are moved in order and are in FIFO sequence

Moving unload to this position increases buffer capacity

(Front view)

Figure 3-9. Continued.

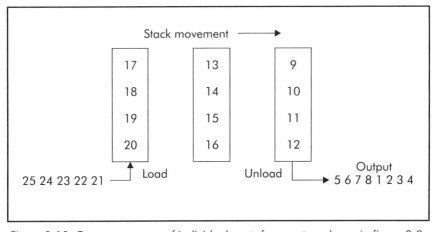

Stack movement ⟶

17	13	9
18	14	10
19	15	11
20	16	12

25 24 23 22 21 ── Load   Unload ── Output 5 6 7 8 1 2 3 4

Figure 3-10. Output sequence of individual parts from system shown in figure 3-9e.

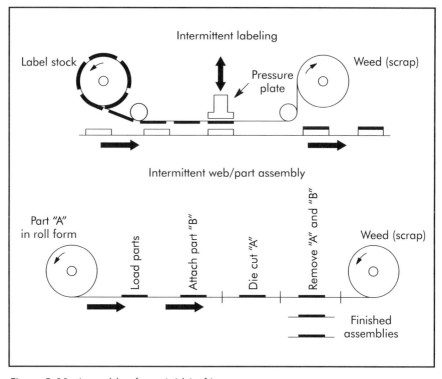

Figure 3-11. Assembly of nonrigid (soft) components.

SPEED RANGE OF TRANSFER METHODS

All of the basic assembly processes or transfer methods have a normal range of operation. After the required machine rate is determined, the various transfer method options can be evaluated. Figure 3-12 provides an overview of the different approaches to automated assembly and the machine rate they normally cover.

Intermittent, in-line continuous, and rotary continuous are all *synchronous transfer methods*, that is, the workstations are synchronized with one another. Power-and-free is a *nonsynchronous transfer method* where each station operates independently from others in the same assembly line. See Chapter 5 for a more detailed description of transfer methods. Figure 3-13 shows a more detailed listing of transfer methods and the typical output range for each.

NUMBER OF COMPONENTS AND OPERATIONS

The total number of components and operations is a major factor in choosing a transfer method. As the number of components and opera-

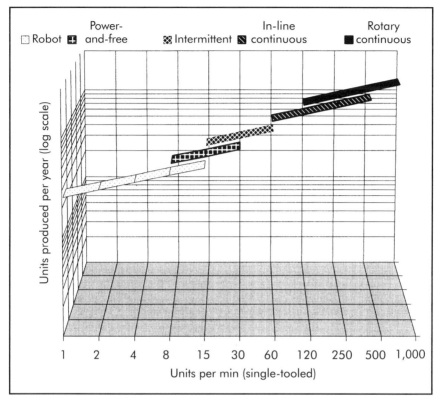

Figure 3-12. Approximate speed ranges of basic transfer methods.

tions increases, machine complexity increases and reliability decreases. The importance of product design for manufacturing becomes clearer when comparing equipment requirements and reliability using a product designed for automated assembly with that of a product designed for manual assembly.

An experienced automation engineer looks at many factors when considering how to assemble a product. Identifying any unusual or difficult processes is usually one of the first steps. Since the possibilities for special processes are unlimited, it is not possible to offer any general references. However, if the assembly processes fall in what could be called "normal automated assembly," a few general references may be worth discussing.

As a practical matter, the more operations there are in an assembly system, the slower the assembly rate. This is because as the number of operations increases, the added complexity makes high speed increasingly difficult. As was discussed earlier in this section, the interdepen-

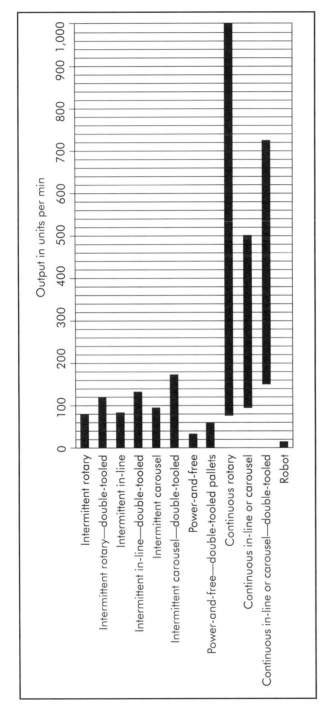

Figure 3-13. Typical speed range of common transfer methods.

dence of operations in a synchronous assembly system makes the system reliability, and therefore effective output, drop as more steps are added. As a result, the number of operations limits the output rate of a synchronous assembly system.

A simple method for comparing the complexity of different assembly systems is to add the number of parts, placements, and process steps. Process steps, such as welding or testing, should be counted since they can be expected to contribute to downtime. Simple verification of a placement can usually be ignored because the contribution to downtime is usually negligible. If the total is greater than 15, strong consideration should be given to separating the processes over two machines with a buffer between them. If the number is low, say five to seven, higher speed methods, such as continuous motion, may be possible. If the number is greater than 20, a nonsynchronous (power-and-free) assembly system should be considered.

Example

A product requires the assembly of five parts. Each part is fed and loaded individually (no subassemblies). During assembly, one staking operation and one test station are required. It is desired to assemble this product on a synchronous assembly machine at a rate of 45 assemblies per minute.

The total number of parts, placements, and processes is twelve, as shown in Table 3-7. Twelve is a reasonable number of parts, placements, and processes for a single synchronous machine. Note that although an assembly system may have four or five value-added operations, the product may be subject to several times this number of transfers or transition points. This is one reason why many assembly machines never achieve a machine run time higher than 70-80%.

The number of operations that can be handled by the different transfer methods varies greatly. Figure 3-14 shows the recommended maximum number of operations for common transfer methods. Double-tooling does not change the recommended maximum. In terms of machine complexity, assembling two products at a time, each containing five steps, is equivalent to assembling one product containing 10 steps.

Table 3-7. Synchronous Machine Capability

Number of parts	5
Number of placements	5
Number of processes	2
Total	12

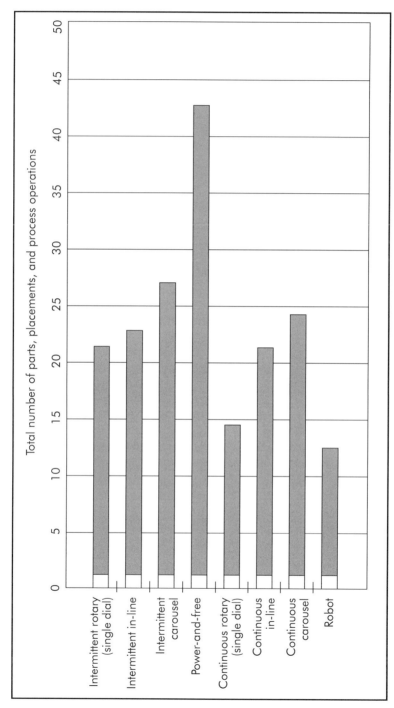

Figure 3-14. Maximum number of parts, placements, and operations for common transfer methods (adapted from Treer 1979).

SUMMARY

A new automated assembly investment must support the strategic business objectives as well as the production needs of the manufacturing organization. Determining production capacity required per machine is one of the first critical decisions because production rate defines which technical options can be considered. Although technical capability will determine the upper process limit, business and competitive strategies must be considered as well as the cost/value of the alternatives.

System reliability is affected not only by equipment design but also by most of the functions involved in production. Maximum reliability and productivity requires optimizing the total system, not just individual functions. Buffers, quick changeover, and minimizing time to restart can be very effective in improving system productivity. System reliability depends on machine speed, time to restart, and reliability of both process operations and incoming parts. An analysis of these factors before the system design is finalized can be very useful in helping to achieve high system reliability.

REFERENCES

Hayes, Robert H., Wheelwright, Steven C., and Clark, Kim B. 1988. *Dynamic Manufacturing*. New York: Free Press: 44.

Nakajima, Seiichi. 1988. *Introduction to TPM—Total Productive Maintenance*. Cambridge, MA: Productivity Press: 21-29.

Riley, Frank J. 1983. *Assembly Automation: A Management Handbook*. New York: Industrial Press: 23.

Treer, Kenneth R. 1979. *Automated Assembly* (Adaptation). Dearborn, MI: Society of Manufacturing Engineers: 162, 173.

The Product

SIMPLIFYING THE PRODUCT

Approximately 80% of a product's cost is fixed during the first 15% of its development cycle. The ultimate manufacturing cost of most products can be reduced by including an automation engineer early in the new product development cycle.

The first step in automating the assembly of an existing product is to evaluate the product for *automated* assembly. Simplifying the product design is essential. The higher the production speed, the more important product simplification is. Assemblies containing 10 or more components will typically be limited to an assembly speed of 60 ppm or less for the reasons discussed in Chapter 3. Complex products often can be reduced into subassemblies, which simplifies the number of operations required of any one machine. For an assembly to be a candidate for very high-speed assembly (that is, 500 ppm or higher), it should have no more than four components. If a time-dependent process (such as ultrasonic welding) is required, the speed of assembly is further limited. Products containing hundreds or even thousands of parts are usually assembled on power-and-free systems. Use of subassemblies is important to minimize complexity and maintain good run time at final assembly. An automation engineer can advise the product development team on various choices affecting manufacturing cost (see "Number of Components and Operations" in Chapter 3).

Getting the parts into the desired position—material handling—is usually the major challenge with high-speed automated assembly. Most problems occur at the static-to-dynamic transitions. Material or component handling becomes increasingly important as either the number of components, cube size, or speed increases.

COMPONENT SIZE EFFECTS

In addition to complexity, size of individual product components also affects assembly speed, as shown in Figure 4-1. Very high-speed assembly is practical for a fairly narrow range of components. When the longest dimension of a component increases beyond 3 or 4 in. (76 or 102

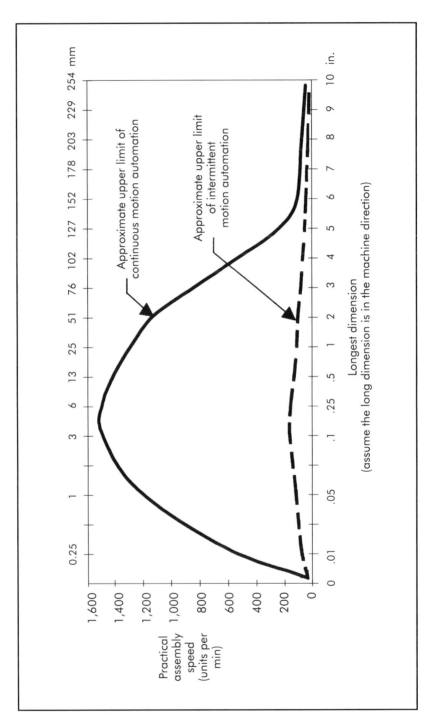

Figure 4-1. Component size versus assembly speed (*discrete components*).

mm), or decreases below .010 in. (0.25 mm), handling becomes increasingly difficult. The smaller dimensions are more commonly found in the manufacture of electrical and electronic products.

The *aspect ratio* (length to width) of a part is also an important consideration in feeding and locating. For example, a part that measures 2.0 × .50 × .50 in. (51 × 13 × 13 mm) is easier to orient than one that is .60 × .50 × .50 in. (15 × 13 × 13 mm). Weight, shape, and other factors, such as rigidity, also influence the practical speed at which a particular component can be handled reliably. Lightweight parts can be particularly troublesome at higher speeds, since they are easily affected by air currents and machine vibration.

Products manufactured from web-fed components can frequently be produced at higher speeds. Diapers, feminine hygiene products, flat-pack disposable batteries for instant film, and others are not only physically larger, but are manufactured at very high rates. Although the speed limits of a web-fed assembly process are even less well defined, Figure 4-2 shows approximate relationships. When combining discrete components with a web-fed process, handling and placement of the discrete component will most likely be the limiting operation.

PRODUCT DESIGN FOR ASSEMBLY

Training courses that specifically address product design for assembly are available. However, these courses are generally limited to hardware assembly, and frequently do not address problems with "soft" products or high-speed assembly. Although these courses offer useful techniques, they are not a substitute for involving the assembly system designer during product design. The person responsible for the assembly system can add a valuable perspective specific to the product being designed.

Involving manufacturing engineers in the product design can pay big dividends in production. In one situation, a team that included both product development and manufacturing engineers developed a product line for relays. An assembled size-1 relay with the cover removed is shown in Figure 4-3. As a result of this cooperative effort, the assembly system is both simple and flexible. The assembly system can assemble any of the four basic product sizes on the same pallet. All four products (a, b, c, and d) are designed with essentially identical working components arranged in the same way and in the same location on all products, as shown in Figure 4-4. Because of the similarity between products, they can be located on the pallet so that the assembly operations are identical for all four products. The assembly system has the flexibility to produce a lot size of one of any of the four product sizes.

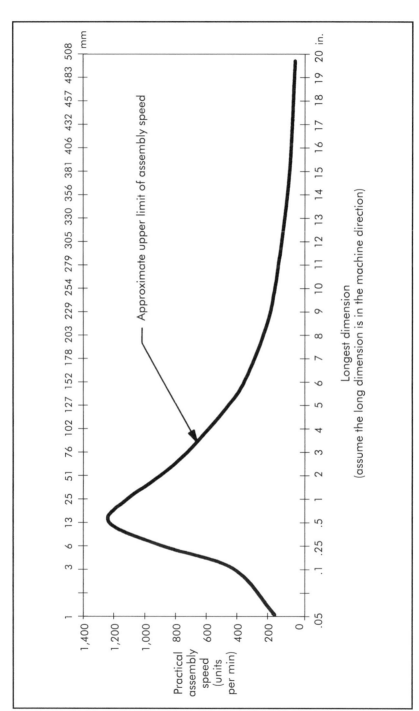

Figure 4-2. Component size versus assembly speed (web-fed).

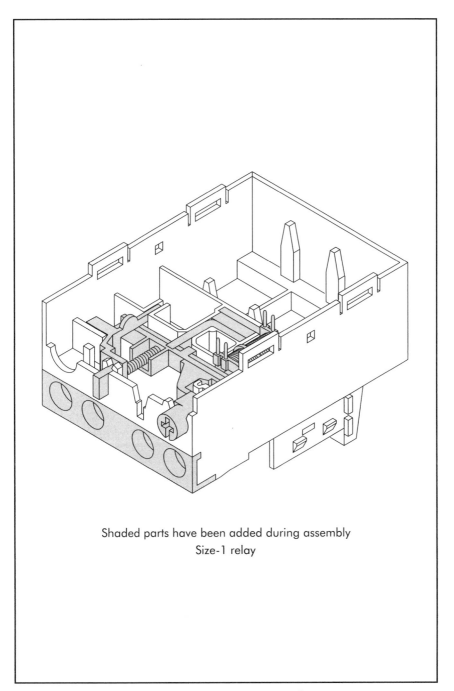

Shaded parts have been added during assembly
Size-1 relay

Figure 4-3. Assembled size-1 relay (courtesy Allen-Bradley).

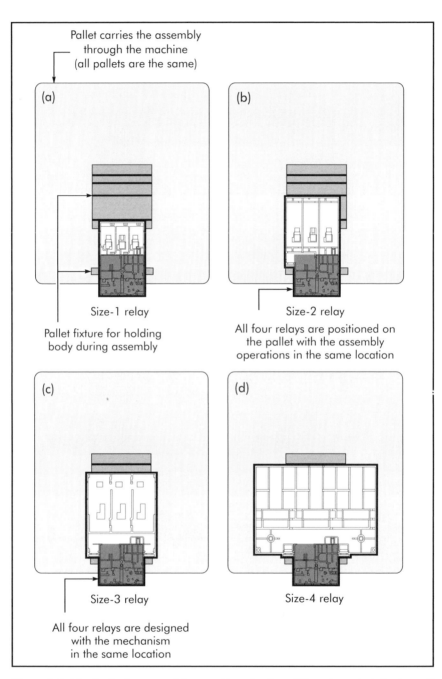

Figure 4-4. Identical relay assembly operations for four different products (a, b, c, d) (courtesy Allen-Bradley).

Another example of a cooperative effort was to improve an ink cartridge. The cartridge was optimized to eliminate parts and simplify the assembly operation. Ink cartridges must allow air to enter as it replaces the volume of ink used. Since rapid pressure changes can affect the print quality, the air entering the cartridge is "metered" by passing it through a bubble generator. The bubble generator creates very small bubbles, minimizing the pressure change caused by each bubble. The original design shown in Figure 4-5 required six parts (bubble generator plate,

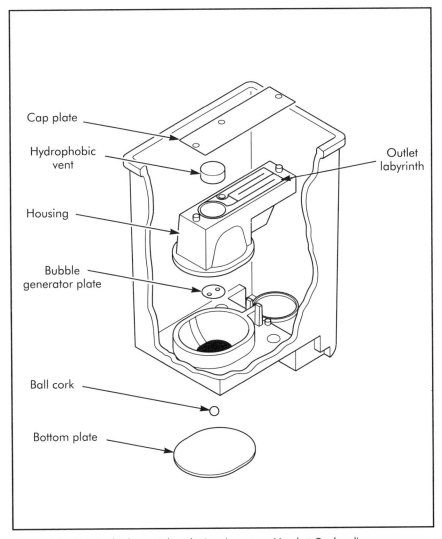

Figure 4-5. Original ink cartridge design (courtesy Hewlett Packard).

housing with labyrinth, hydrophobic vent, cap plate, ball cork, and bottom plate). Four parts were assembled from the top and two from the bottom, requiring the assembly to be turned over. This design also required that the housing be partially filled with deionized water to wet the hydrophobic vent.

The newer design, shown in Figure 4-6, has the labyrinth molded into the body and requires only two additional parts (ball cork and bottom plate). By eliminating the hydrophobic vent, the process step of injecting deionized water was also eliminated. In the new design, an annulus around the ball acts as the bubble generator. Also, note that

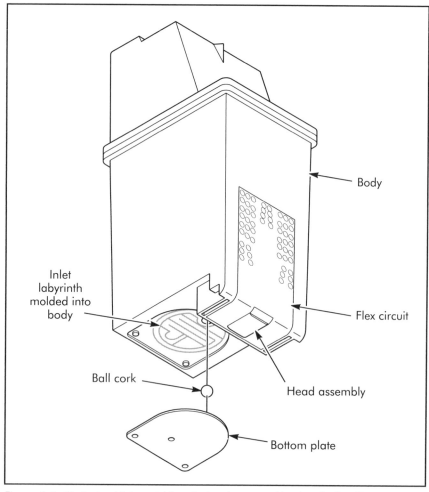

Figure 4-6. Optimized ink cartridge design (courtesy Hewlett Packard).

the location of the parts in the new design is on the outside surface instead of inside the body, making assembly easier. Note that both the old and new ink cartridges contained additional parts that are not shown for the sake of simplicity.

As stated earlier in this chapter, component handling is often the biggest assembly challenge. Delicate and/or irregularly shaped components, which are susceptible to damage when stacked in magazines, can be handled by adding a "handling" feature. The handling feature is removed during assembly and does not affect product performance. Figures 4-7 and 4-8 are examples of this technique used in the manufacture of a disk film product.

Figure 4-9 illustrates how product design can facilitate improved quality by allowing automated on-line inspection. The packaging artwork was modified to allow automatic inspection using machine vision.

The direction of assembly or the direction of insertion of parts is extremely important. A product that can be assembled entirely with vertical motions is likely to be accomplished with a simpler, less costly machine than one that requires a combination of vertical and horizontal motions. Generally, top-down vertical insertions are best.

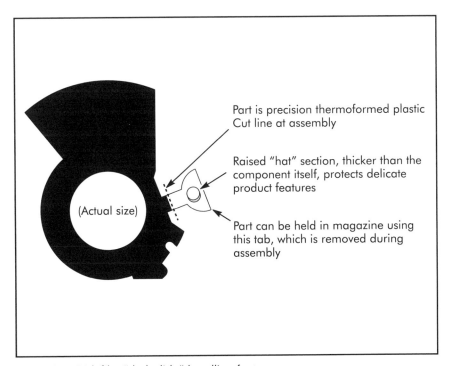

Figure 4-7. Disk film "dark slide" handling feature.

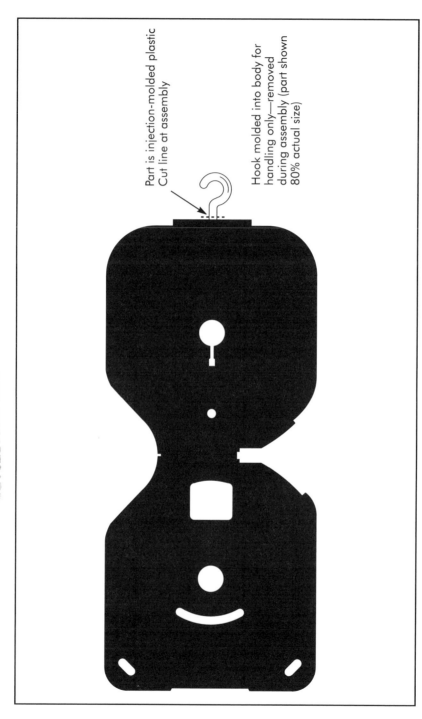

Part is injection-molded plastic
Cut line at assembly

Hook molded into body for handling only—removed during assembly (part shown 80% actual size)

Figure 4-8. Disk film "body" handling feature.

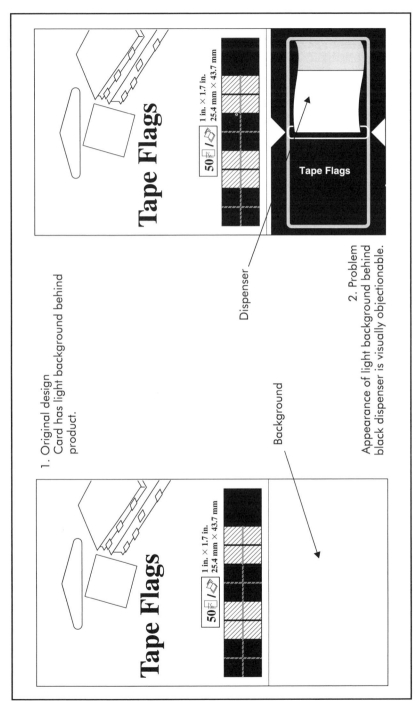

Figure 4-9. Tape flag back card design to facilitate on-line inspection (courtesy 3M).

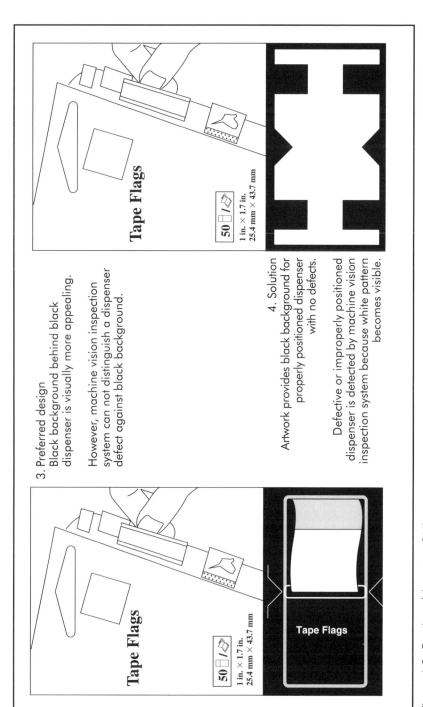

3. Preferred design
Black background behind black dispenser is visually more appealing.

However, machine vision inspection system can not distinguish a dispenser defect against black background.

4. Solution
Artwork provides black background for properly positioned dispenser with no defects.

Defective or improperly positioned dispenser is detected by machine vision inspection system because white pattern becomes visible.

Figure 4-9. Continued (courtesy 3M).

FASTENING METHODS FOR AUTOMATION

Fastening methods for high-volume automated assembly are quite limited. As speed increases, the options for fastening decrease. Ultrasonic welding is a popular method of joining plastic parts. However, the time required for ultrasonic welding does not lend itself to very high-speed manufacturing. Snap-together components are preferred for high-speed assembly. But other methods, such as cold staking, are acceptable in many situations. Table 4-1 lists various fastening methods and typical attachment times. Figure 4-10 shows attachment data and Figure 4-11 shows cycle-rate data. Both figures use data from Table 4-1 and present it in graph form. Figures 4-12 through 4-15 show examples of typical fastening methods.

SUMMARY

Products designed for manufacturing efficiency provide a business much greater opportunity for competitive success. Simplifying the product, reducing the number of components, using preferred assembly methods, and designing components to be handled automatically can have a major impact on manufacturing efficiency. Simplifying the product reduces the cost of the production equipment and the ongoing cost of manufacturing it. Involving an automation engineer early in the product design process helps ensure that the product can be manufactured efficiently and at the highest possible quality level.

The product itself and how it is designed dictates the options available for manufacture. Chapter 5 discusses this relationship and the various assembly processes.

Table 4-1. Fastening Methods and Attachment Times

	Fastening Method	Typical Attachment Time (milliseconds)	Typical Maximum Rate* (cycles/min)	Typical Applications	Notes
1	Crimp	50-1,000	1,000+†	Metallic and some plastics	Limited by thickness of part to be deformed.
2	Press fit	60-2,000	1,000+†	Combination of various materials	Adequate support must be provided at pressing station.
3	Resistance (spot weld)	60-3,000	1,000+†	Metallic	It is desirable for both parts to be the same metal and similar thickness. Larger parts, such as studs, may have protrusions to concentrate current.
4	Pressure-sensitive adhesive	60-1,000	1,000	Combination of various materials	High cycle rate operations require PSA carrier to be pre-applied to a web-fed liner.
5	Staple	60-500	1,000	Combination of various materials	Operation is generally performed in a static condition.
6	Hot melt adhesive	60-5,000	1,000	Combination of various materials	Applicable to nonload-bearing bonds only; costly equipment enhancements are required for dry/cure times necessary for high cycle rates.
7	Screwed-on part	100-2,000	800	Plastic or metal caps	

* Single-tooled.
† Higher rates tend to be for very small parts, such as those typical in the electronics industry.

Table 4-1. Fastening Methods and Attachment Times (continued)

	Fastening Method	Typical Attachment Time (milliseconds)	Typical Maximum Rate* (cycles/min)	Typical Applications	Notes
8	Snap fit	100-500	400	Plastic or paper	Attachment time is limited only by frictional interface between parts and dynamic limits of material deflection.
9	Cold stake	200-1,000	160	Plastic or light-duty metallic	Materials must exhibit adequate plastic flow properties.[††]
10	Ultrasonic weld	400-3,000	60	Plastic, fabric, or film	Higher rates may be attainable if welding is performed as a converting process, that is, while material is still in web form.[††]
11	Screw	500 - 3,000	60	Plastic or metallic	Should generally be avoided unless disassembly is required.
12	Spin/friction weld	750 - 4,000	60	Plastics	Circular interface between parts is required; part size is inertia-limited. Accurate control of rpm and number of rotations may be required to maintain consistent welds.
13	Other adhesive/ solvent weld	1,000-30,000	60	Combination of various materials	Cure time of appropriate adhesive can vary greatly based upon material being bonded and load conditions encountered.
14	Orbital rivet	1,000-15,000	20	Plastic or metallic	Assembly rates are a function of the material deformation properties.

[††] Cold stake and ultrasonics can be combined if material has too much memory for cold staking alone.

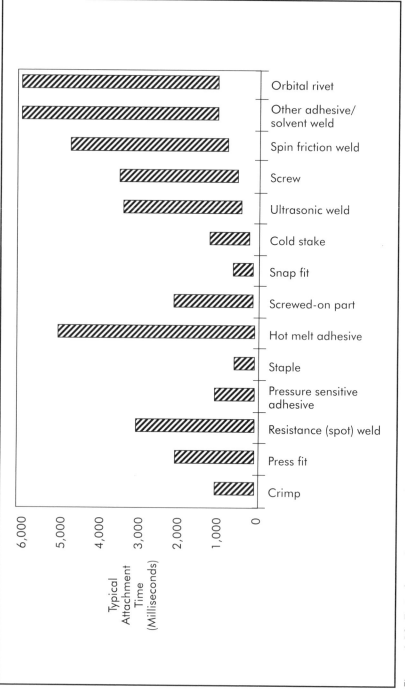

Figure 4-10. Typical attachment time for common fastening methods.

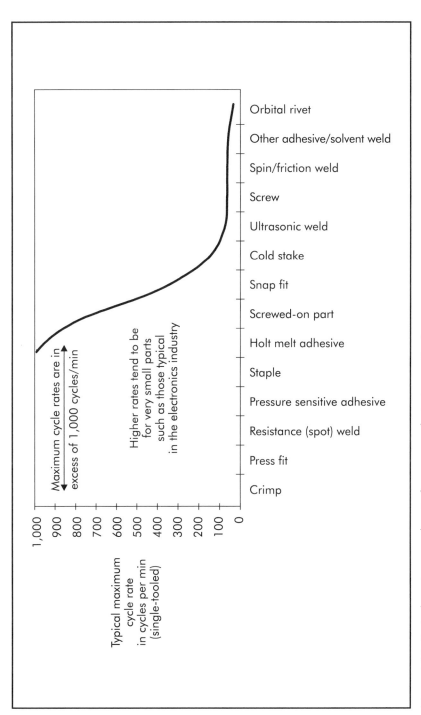

Figure 4-11. Typical maximum cycle rate for common fastening methods.

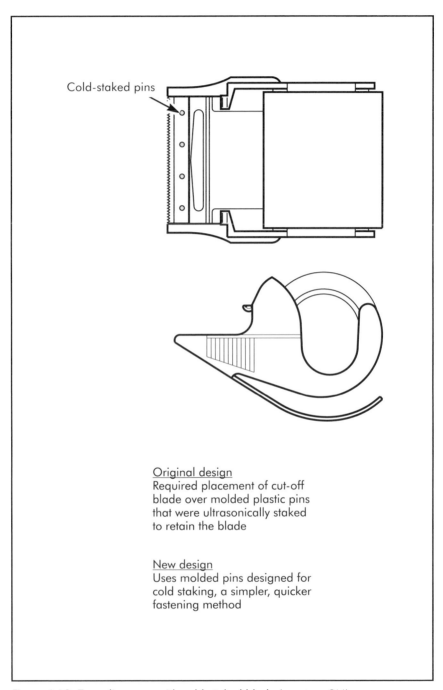

Cold-staked pins

Original design
Required placement of cut-off
blade over molded plastic pins
that were ultrasonically staked
to retain the blade

New design
Uses molded pins designed for
cold staking, a simpler, quicker
fastening method

Figure 4-12. Tape dispenser with cold-staked blade (courtesy 3M).

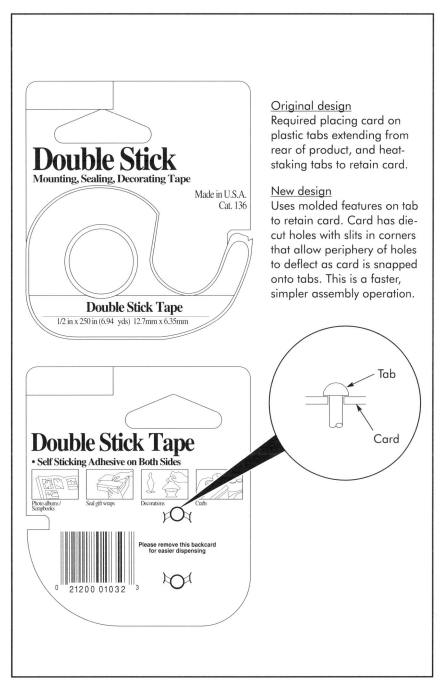

Figure 4-13. Double stick tape dispenser with snap-on back card (courtesy 3M).

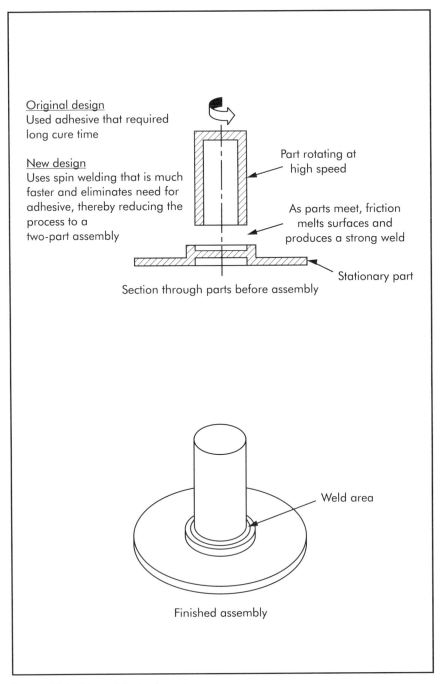

Figure 4-14. Spin weld attachment.

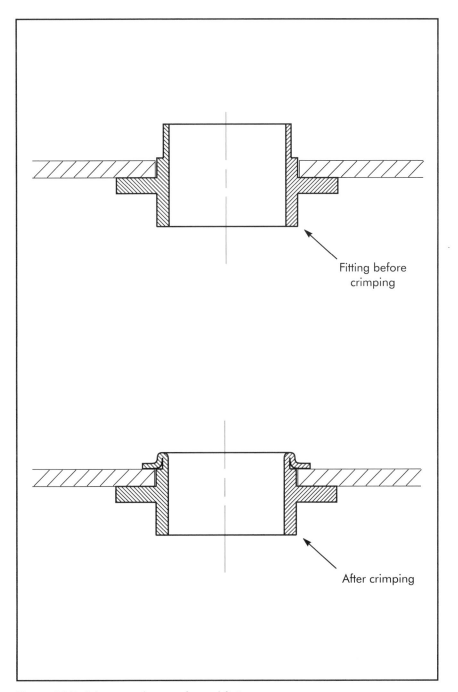

Figure 4-15. Crimp attachment of metal fitting.

5

Assembly Processes

TRANSFER METHODS FOR ASSEMBLY PROCESSES

Transfer method refers to the manner of moving the product through various stations where tasks are performed. Each of the three basic assembly processes—intermittent, power-and-free (nonsynchronous) and continuous—can be accomplished using several approaches, as shown in Figure 5-1.

Some products can be assembled in part or totally from components supplied in web form. The assembly process in this case corresponds to an intermittent or continuous in-line process. Assembly methods are unique for each product and process.

Assembling both web-fed and discrete parts on a single machine requires knowledge of both areas. Assembly problems for such components are product-related and are not covered in this book. Several hybrid and special assembly processes are discussed later in this chapter. Refer to Chapter 3 for more information on typical speed ranges for various transfer methods and reliability information related to the number of operations.

INTERMITTENT TRANSFER METHODS

Because intermittent transfer methods (also referred to as intermittent-motion assembly or IMA) require that the part be moved from station to station, the "time on target" available for actual work is severely restricted. Inertial forces usually limit the speed of the index portion of the cycle. Consequently, single-tooled, intermittent transfer systems are generally limited to around 60 parts per minute (ppm). Although intermittent assembly machines can be designed to run in excess of 150 ppm, this is not common and usually applies only to small products and highly engineered systems. As the spacing between nests increases, index speed (and output) is reduced.

The accuracy of the index is often an important consideration. On rotary tables, where the tooling is located at a 6-in. (15-cm) radius or less and a high-quality index drive is used, an index accuracy of ±.002

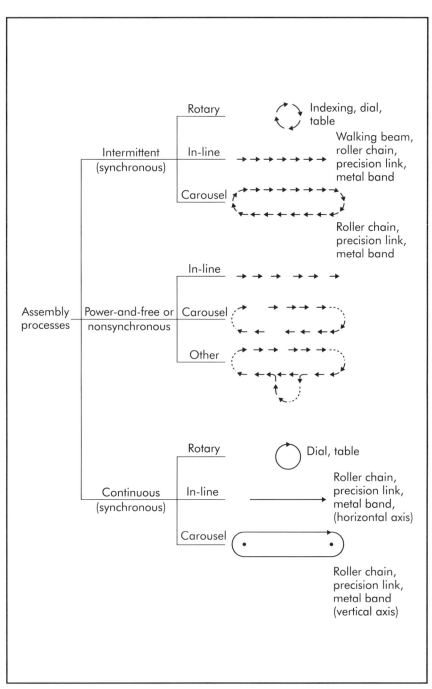

Figure 5-1. Transfer methods for assembly processes (adapted from Treer 1979).

in. (0.05 mm) is normally attainable. If more accuracy is required, shot-pinning is necessary. *Shot-pinning* is a more accurate locating method in which a tapered pin or plug is driven into a tapered hole or slot on the tooling to accurately locate the tooling during each dwell period.

Intermittent Rotary

Intermittent rotary transfer is one of the most common and least costly methods of transferring product, as shown in Figure 5-2. Frequently referred to as a rotary table, this approach depends on an index drive to provide the desired advance and dwell.

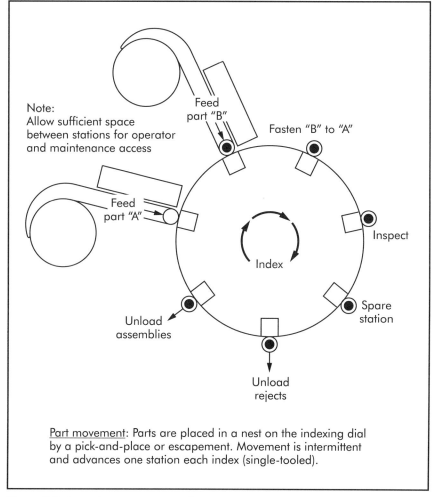

Figure 5-2. Intermittent rotary transfer.

Intermittent In-line

Intermittent in-line transfer, as shown by Figure 5-3, requires roller chain, precision links, or a steel band to maintain accurate spacing between the product pallets. The product is carried on pallets held in a track, and the system is moved by an indexing drive, as shown in Figure 5-4.

The system can be designed with a vertical axis or a horizontal axis, as shown in Figure 5-3. One of the major advantages of in-line configuration, when compared to a rotary table, is the additional space available for mechanisms and maintenance access. One disadvantage of the horizontal axis configuration is that less than half of the pallets are being used at any time. This can be significant if costly pallet tooling is required.

Roller chain is less expensive than precision links or steel band, but is also less accurate. Roller chain wears and stretches during use, changing the distance between pallets and, therefore, is not recommended. To maintain reasonable alignment between pallets and workstations, the stretch in the chain must be anticipated and compensated for. One method of compensation is to make the pallets compliant, so that they can be moved forward a small amount relative to the chain they are attached to. This will allow the workstation to align correctly. Compliant pallets are also useful in other situations where alignment is critical.

A precision link system wears far less than roller chain. Steel band is the most stable of the indexing methods. The longer the in-line chain link or belt, the more wear and stretch affects alignment between pallets and workstations.

Indexing Mechanisms

Although a number of mechanisms can be used to generate intermittent motion for driving dial or in-line machines, only two are generally found in assembly machines. These are the Geneva mechanism and barrel-cam mechanism, as shown in Figure 5-4.

The Geneva mechanism is the simplest to manufacture because it requires only the machining of plates. However, because of its limitations, it is generally not recommended. The major disadvantage of the Geneva mechanism is that its high speed motion characteristics are poor, due to step changes in the acceleration profile. This leads to infinite jerk. A second disadvantage is that required clearances in the mechanism lead to backlash.

The barrel-cam mechanism offers careful control so that motion is smooth and jerk is always finite. Also, the use of cam followers allows the barrel-cam mechanism to be preloaded so that backlash is dramatically

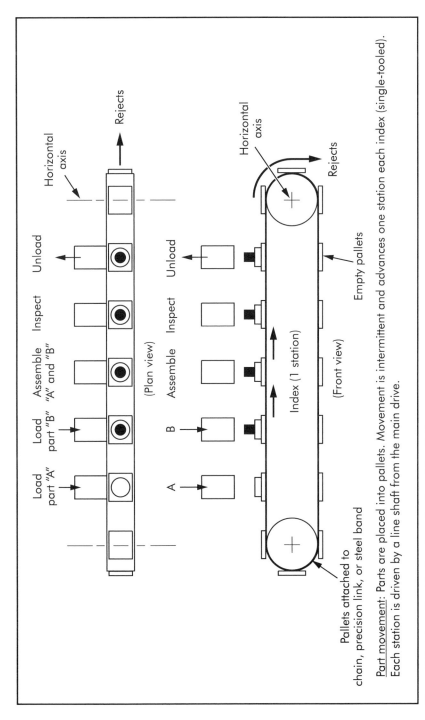

Figure 5-3. Intermittent in-line transfer (precision link).

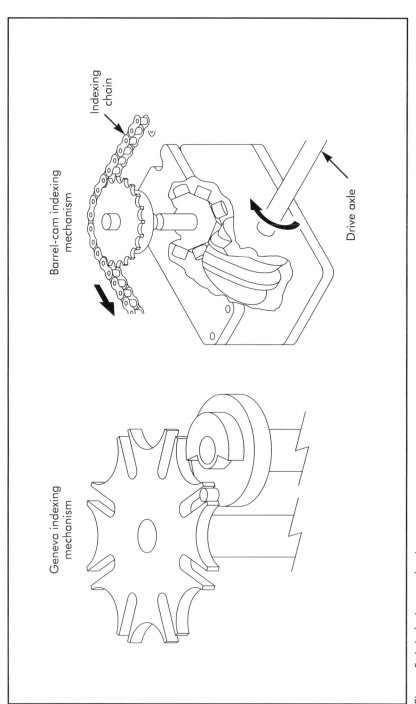

Figure 5-4. Indexing mechanisms.

reduced. Use of barrel-cam mechanisms is generally recommended on any automation machine where intermittent motion is required.

Intermittent In-line (Walking Beam)

The walking beam method of product transfer is shown in Figure 5-5. All parts in the track are moved simultaneously. They are picked up and moved to the next nest or pushed along the track. The pusher then retracts and returns to home position for the next cycle. The walking beam is a very useful transfer method for certain automation systems. However, when prototyping the critical process areas, consider the transfer itself as a process worth proving with a prototype. Picking up a part from one station and transferring it to the next is a very dynamic process. Unless well thought out, it can result in extensive debug efforts and possible redesign to solve very basic problems.

Consider the dynamics of the actual part transfer, particularly with small, light, or resilient parts. The impact between the transfer nest and the part can cause the part to bounce out of the tooling or become misaligned so that it will not locate properly in the next station's tooling. This problem is compounded when high speeds are involved. Consider holding the part in place positively, rather than relying on gravity.

When handling difficult parts, analyze the dynamics of the walking beam mechanism. Smooth, low-velocity contact and release of the part may be required to maintain reliable part control. If the tooling is cantilevered very far from the walking beam drive, consider using two walking beam drives in tandem or find a way to support the beam to maintain the desired motion along its entire length.

In one case, where both impact and speed had to be resolved during debug, about four months were lost. While the machine was very successful in the end, better up-front engineering and analysis could have saved considerable time and money.

Intermittent Carousel

Figure 5-6 shows an intermittent carousel transfer, which is similar in operation to intermittent in-line transfer. In an in-line system, the conveyor moves about a horizontal axis and is often referred to as an "axis horizontal" system. A carousel is an "axis vertical" configuration. Tasks can be performed from both sides of the transfer conveyor.

To increase production rate, any transfer system can be multiple-tooled to load and assemble multiple parts during a single index cycle. Figure 5-7 shows one type of intermittent double-tooled carousel where pallets are advanced two positions at a time. To provide sufficient access for operators and maintenance, it may be necessary to space out the workstations and allow idle pallets in between.

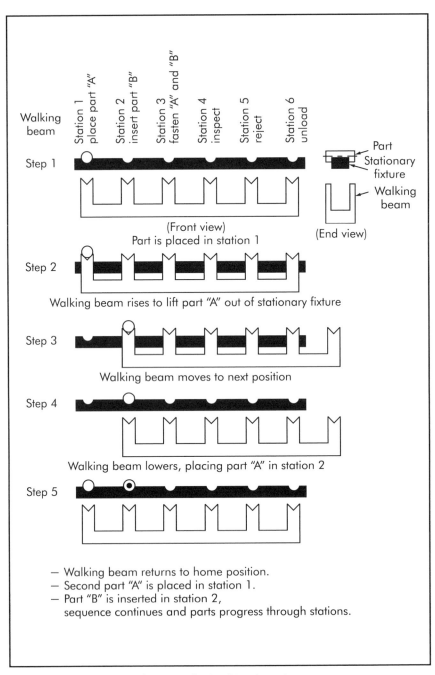

Figure 5-5. Intermittent in-line transfer (walking beam).

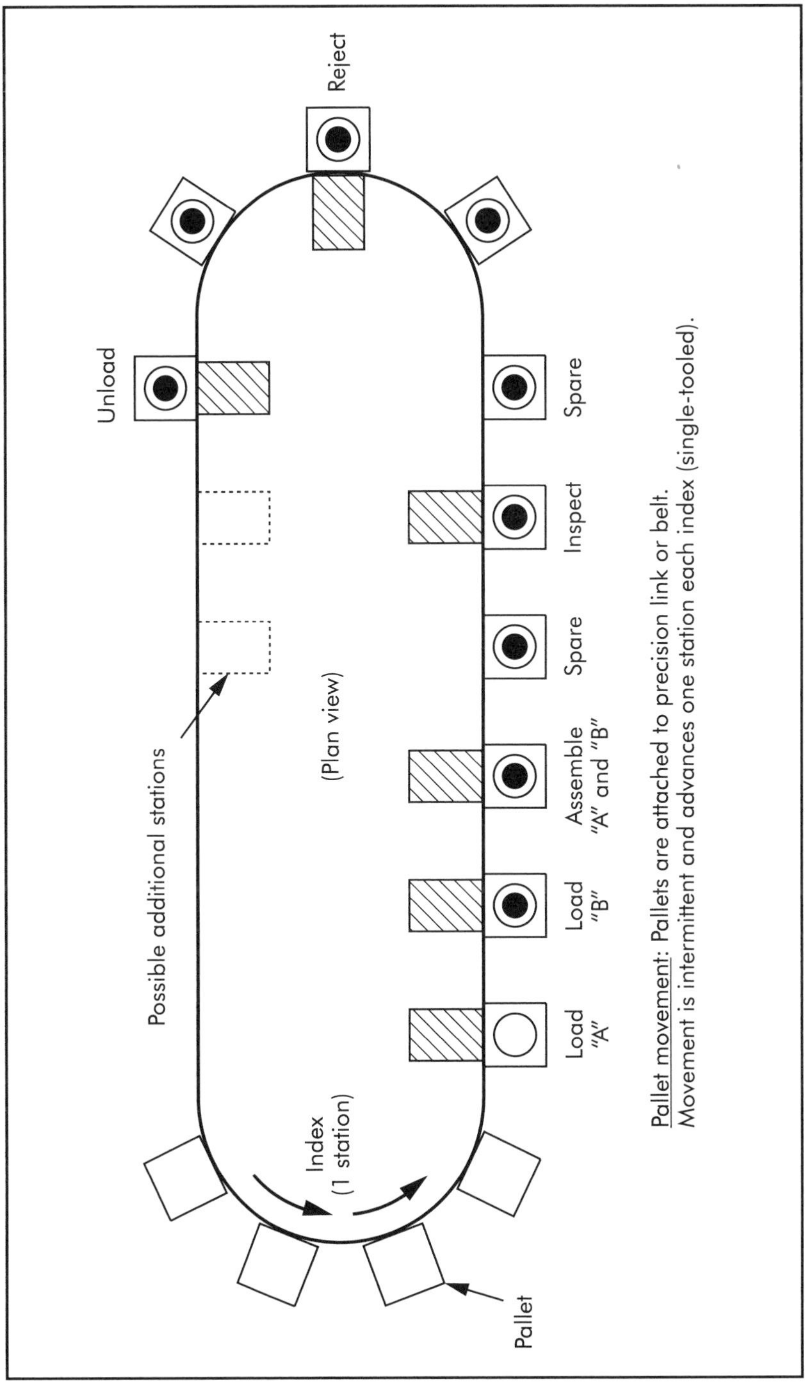

Figure 5-6. Intermittent carousel transfer.

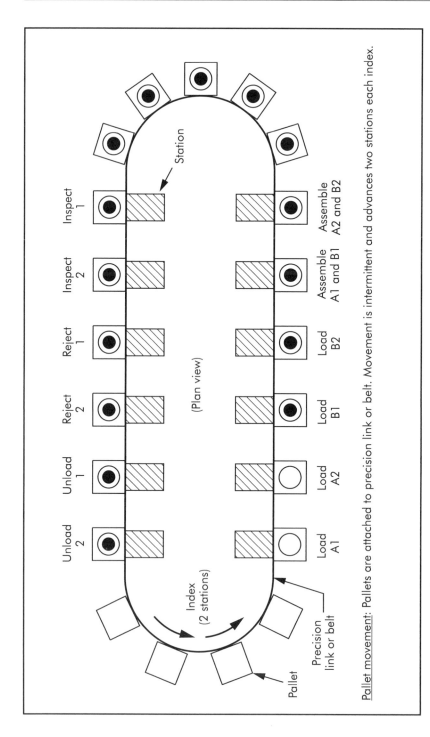

Figure 5-7. Intermittent double-tooled carousel transfer.

POWER-AND-FREE

A power-and-free nonsynchronous transfer system uses pallets to carry the product, as shown in Figure 5-8. Pallets are free to ride between workstations on a continuously running, powered belt. On arrival at a workstation, a pallet is captured and located in a fixed position while work is performed. When the work is complete, the pallet is free again to ride on the powered belt to the next workstation. The first step toward automating a manual assembly line is frequently a simple power-and-free system. Each manual assembly station operator removes a workpiece from the moving conveyor, performs the required task, and replaces it on the conveyor. Power-and-free systems can link a series of manual stations, automatic stations, or some of each, as shown in Figure 5-8. Power-and-free systems are frequently used to assemble families of products: products with a common base and variable parts applied to the base. This is shown in Figure 5-9.

Pallets can be coded using a combination of holes or pins in the pallet that are read by sensors at each station or by programmable coding devices. Bar codes can be affixed to either the pallet or product itself and read at each station. Many varieties of programmable coding devices are available that use magnetic, radio frequency, and other methods to code and read information specific to each pallet. Lot sizes of one with no changeover are common with these systems.

More complex products or product families with more variables can be accommodated with side loops, as shown in Figure 5-10. Side loops can also accommodate manual tasks, such as testing, inspection, and rework.

Power-and-free systems must be designed with consideration for the following:

- Pallet transfer time between stations;
- Pallet acceleration and deceleration times; and
- Pallet shot-pin time, if required.

Power-and-free systems generally run at speeds below 30 ppm. However, an increase in production can be obtained by multiple-tooling each pallet. For example, a pallet could be multiple-tooled to hold three products, as shown in Figure 5-11. Once the pallet is in position at a workstation, it can be indexed or repositioned rapidly for each of the three products. Repositioning a single pallet is usually done much more quickly than changing pallets, thereby increasing the production rate. Rates of 60 ppm or higher can be obtained using this approach. Figures 5-12 and 5-13 show pallets designed to allow access from above and below the product.

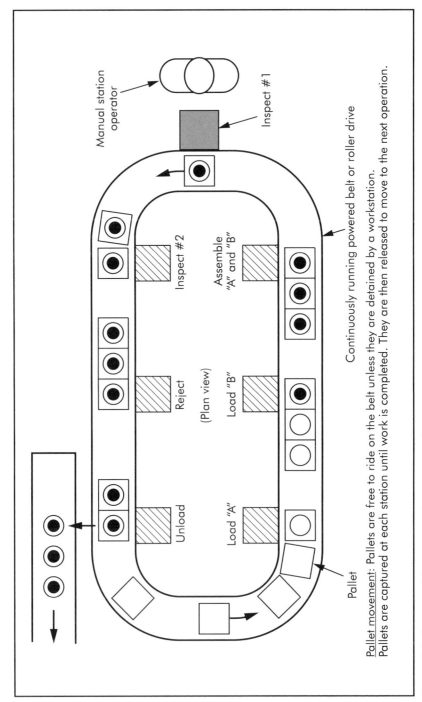

Figure 5-8. Power-and-free nonsynchronous transfer.

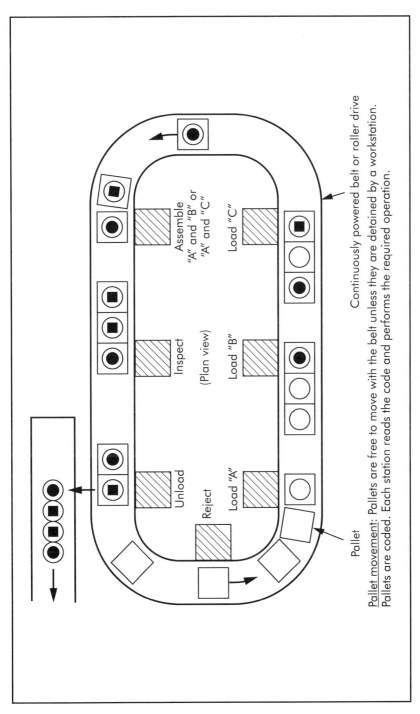

Figure 5-9. Power-and-free nonsynchronous transfer (family of products).

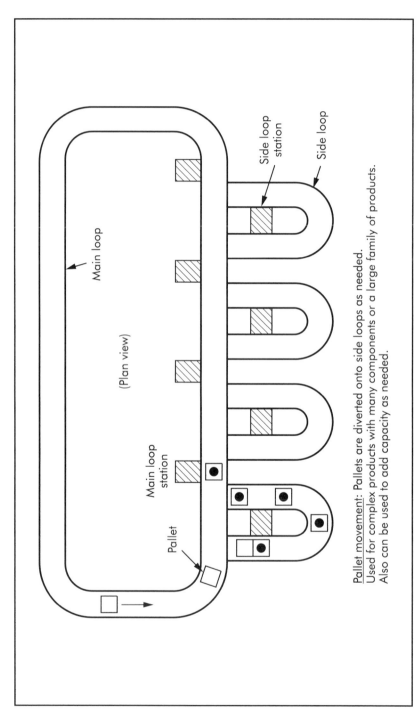

Figure 5-10. Power-and-free nonsynchronous transfer with side loops.

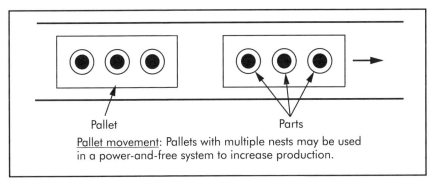

Figure 5-11. Power-and-free transfer (multiple nests).

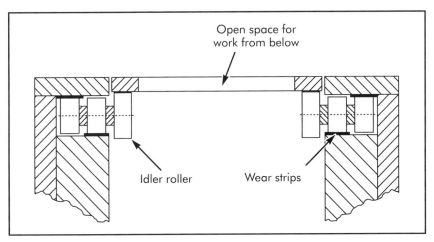

Figure 5-12. Power-and-free transfer for dual-access pallets (Treer 1979).

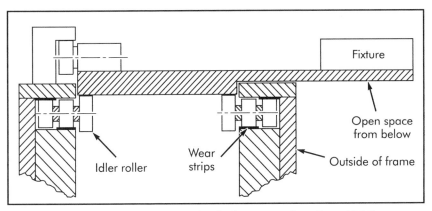

Figure 5-13. Power-and-free transfer for dual-access pallets (Treer 1979).

CONTINUOUS-MOTION ASSEMBLY (CMA)

Whereas intermittent motion and power-and-free systems allow each operation to be performed while the product is stationary, continuous motion requires that work be performed while the product is moving. This requires very different techniques than those used for working on a stationary product. However, some CMA techniques allow a much longer "time on target" than intermittent approaches and provide smoother, gentler product handling. This reduces equipment wear and can result in a more reliable machine. With CMA, rates of hundreds of cycles per minute often can be achieved.

There are two basic approaches to continuous-motion processing:

1. Move the workstation tooling with the product; and
2. Accomplish the operation as the product moves by.

Continuous Rotary

The oldest approach to CMA is the rotary table, as shown in Figure 5-14. Parts are fed onto a rotary table where workstations travel with the parts and perform required tasks. Generally, one rotary table can accomplish a single assembly operation.

If a second assembly operation is required, the product is transferred to a second rotary table. Small and medium-sized products that are generally cylindrical and can utilize vertical assembly motions are good candidates for rotary CMA assembly. Bottles, ammunition, spark plugs, and electrical connectors are examples.

Some products with more than two parts can be assembled on a single continuous rotary transfer dial. Figure 5-15 shows how a three-part product might be assembled on a continuous rotary transfer dial with upper and lower tooling.

Continuous-motion systems are more common with established, high-volume processes, such as food canning and packaging, beverage canning and bottling, disposable diapers and feminine hygiene and tobacco products. It is very useful to observe the equipment and techniques used for such product manufacture and replicate those techniques when appropriate.

When product volumes are in excess of 10 million per year, and where the number of components and operations is low (five or less), CMA is a viable candidate. This is often the case with disposable products. Production rates above 60 ppm (single-tooled) generally require a continuous-motion approach.

It should be noted, however, that frequent changeovers necessitated by a wide variety of product variations (other than simple changes transparent to the machine) can undermine the benefits of high-speed assembly.

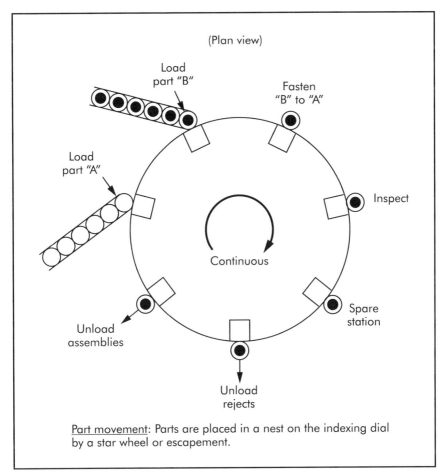

Figure 5-14. Continuous rotary transfer (two-part assembly).

Continuous In-line or Carousel

When product volume warrants looking at CMA, but product design does not lend itself to the rotary table approach, consider in-line or carousel CMA, as shown in Figure 5-16. In an in-line continuous system, the conveyor moves about a horizontal axis. A carousel is an "axis vertical" system, but is otherwise very similar in advantages and challenges to the in-line style and, therefore, will not be discussed here.

In-line or carousel CMA systems are the most advanced assembly transfer methods and employ many techniques not used in other types of systems. The process stations and transfer drive for a continuous in-line system should be driven from a common drive to maintain timing.

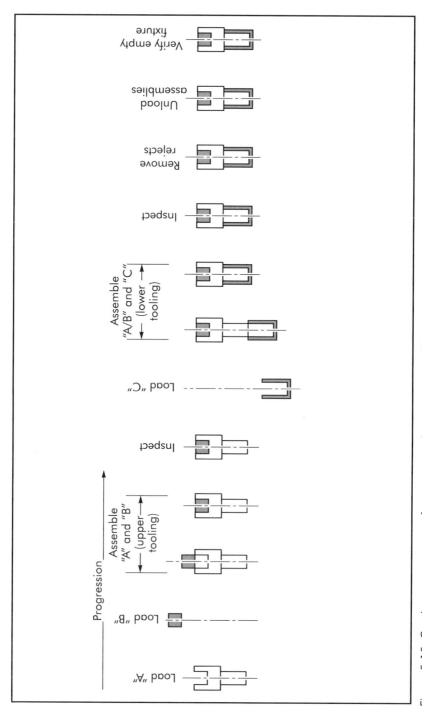

Figure 5-15. Continuous rotary transfer sequence (three-part assembly).

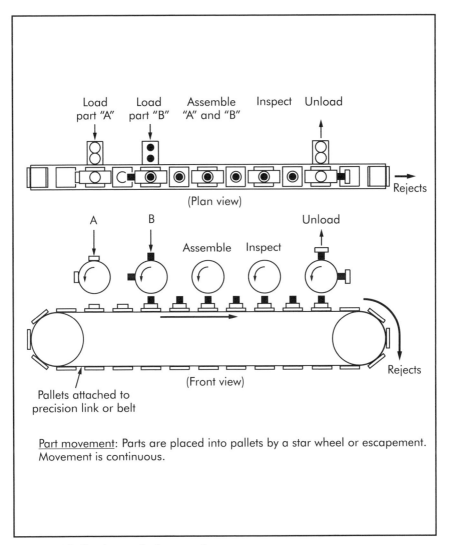

Figure 5-16. Continuous in-line transfer.

Because the product is moving continuously at a constant speed in a straight line, matching its motion with a rotary placement or process operation can be difficult. Compliant pallets offer one way to gain a speed match between linear product motion and the rotary motion of a part being loaded.

Only a few assembly processes (fastening methods) are appropriate for high-speed, in-line CMA assembly. These include simple placement, snap together, and crimping as described in Chapter 4.

Ultrasonic welding is frequently used for assembling plastic components, but it can be too slow for high-speed CMA (above 100 ppm). Some slower assembly processes, including ultrasonic welding, can be accommodated—up to a point—by using a reciprocating bank of welding units or a hybrid technique for indexing the product.

HYBRID ASSEMBLY TECHNIQUES

Hybrid systems are actually forms of indexed multiple tooling and, although they can be very useful, are less desirable than truly continuous techniques. However, when an assembly operation or placement cannot be accomplished in a continuous process, consider techniques that maintain continuous transfer in the base machine while allowing intermittent operations where required.

One technique for combining intermittent and continuous motion is shown in Figure 5-17. With this system, the product is stopped intermittently on one side, while there is continuous product movement on the other. One commercially available version of this concept is the Overton Engine™. The concept is analogous to using a dancer in a web process to stop the web momentarily. Another technique is to combine a power-and-free system with a continuous in-line conveyor, as shown in Figure 5-18.

Hybrid techniques, although useful in special situations, are speed-limited by the intermittent section. A multiple-tooled intermittent-transfer system may accomplish the same task with less complexity.

ROBOTICS

Robotics generates a great deal of interest, but has received slow acceptance in manufacturing. Robots are used extensively in the auto industry for assembly, welding, and painting. They have also found use in machining centers for inserting and removing parts from machine tools and in the assembly of VCRs, watches, and similar consumer products. However, for the assembly of high volume products, robots are generally used only for multiple-part material handling. They are typically too slow or not cost-effective for assembly of high-volume products. However, they should be considered where a very high degree of flexibility is required.

One technology that has tremendous potential in the lower volume manufacturing arena is vision-aided robotics. Combining machine vision with a robot enables a system to adapt to random part orientation, detect defects, and perform other functions, such as quality inspections. Although limited in speed, a vision-aided robot is extremely flexible and should be considered for startup products or where many variations must be accommodated.

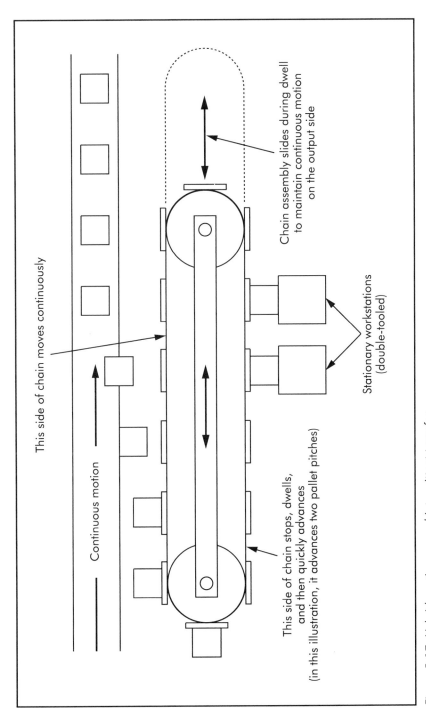

This side of chain moves continuously

Continuous motion

This side of chain stops, dwells,
and then quickly advances
(in this illustration, it advances two pallet pitches)

Stationary workstations
(double-tooled)

Chain assembly slides during dwell
to maintain continuous motion
on the output side

Figure 5-17. *Hybrid continuous and intermittent transfer.*

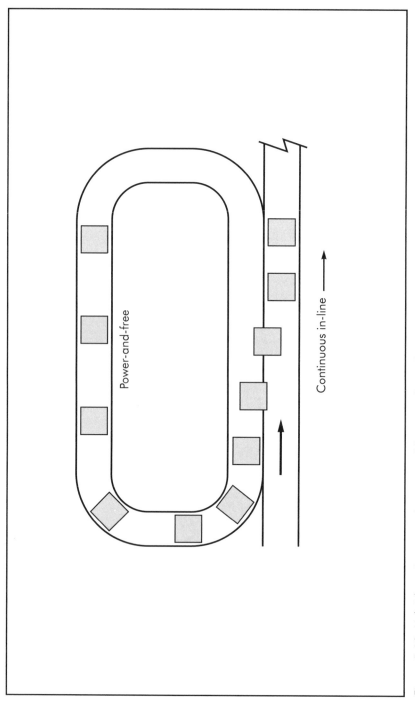

Figure 5-18. Hybrid continuous and power-and-free transfer (in-line conveyor).

SUMMARY

The three basic assembly processes or transfer methods have several variations. Each method is best suited to certain types of products. The assembly of a specific product is often compatible with only a few of the transfer methods. Sometimes, only a few transfer methods support specific business goals, such as lowest cost, multiple product variations or flexibility. An understanding of the strengths and weaknesses of each method is necessary to determine the best choice for the particular product and business goal. Once the best transfer method has been determined, the biggest challenge often becomes material handling, which is addressed in the next chapter.

REFERENCE

Treer, Kenneth R. 1979. *Automated Assembly* (Adaptation). Dearborn, MI: Society of Manufacturing Engineers: 127, 152.

6

Component Feeding

GENERAL CONSIDERATIONS

In many automated assembly operations, the actual assembly processes are relatively straightforward. The real challenge is often in delivering the parts to the assembly site reliably, correctly oriented, and at the required rate. Feeding systems are frequently treated as peripheral to the assembly system, but they are actually an essential and critical element. Component jams in feed bowls, feed tracks, and escapements account for significant unscheduled downtime in many systems. Therefore, make proper selection and design of feeding systems a high priority.

A considerable amount of published resources are available on component feeding and orientation. However, as with most aspects of assembly, these sources do not generally deal with high speeds. Some sources describe systems that code parts by shape and feature. Theoretically, there are methods of determining the likely stable state of different part shapes. Computer programs are available to assist in this analysis and can be useful if complete analysis of a part is desired (Boothroyd 1983).

Feeding devices are usually purchased from a supplier and assembled into the manufacturing system at the shop or at the final plant location. Acceptance of the feed device usually takes place at the feed device supplier's location. Chapter 10 outlines procedures that can help determine acceptance of a feed system. For example, it is good practice to use virgin parts for the acceptance run. Parts that have circulated through a feed system may have the flash worn off, which will make them behave differently than virgin parts.

COMPONENT FEEDING METHODS

These are the basic methods of supplying components to an assembly operation:

- Bulk—parts are loose (not oriented) in a container;
- Magazine—parts are pre-oriented in at least one axis, and are contained in a sleeve, on a rod, or by some other means;
- Roll or bandolier—parts are captured in, attached to, or are a component of a continuous web that is rolled up on a core or layered zigzag fashion (like folded, tractor-fed computer paper) in a container;
- Manufactured on-line—part manufacturing is linked to in-line assembly with or without in-line accumulation; or
- Flexible—machine vision is used to locate parts and determine their orientation, then a robot is directed to pick up the appropriate part.

Bulk Feed

Bulk is, by far, the most common method for feeding components. Bulk-fed parts are dumped from their shipping containers into a hopper or directly into the feeding device. A hopper is often necessary to allow the feed system to operate at optimum efficiency or when the feed device is not large enough to hold a sufficient number of parts. The hopper automatically meters the parts to the feeder as they are needed.

Parts supplied in bulk typically have higher defect rates and contain more debris than those supplied by other methods. Minimal handling is required to get parts from the source (mold or press) into the shipping container, but there is little opportunity to detect defects. Therefore, parts delivered in bulk must be qualified so quality level is maintained, and bulk feed systems must be designed to tolerate some amount of debris and out-of-specification parts.

The transition from manual assembly to automatic assembly usually leads to improved input part quality because defects become more evident.

The two most common feeders are vibratory and centrifugal. Vibratory feeders are generally used for small- to medium-sized parts at slow to moderate feed rates. The general reference for calculating the feed rate for vibratory feeders is 250 in. (635 cm or 6.3 m) per minute. Centrifugal feeders are more appropriate for handling larger parts at moderate to high speeds. The general reference for calculating the feed rate for centrifugal feeders is 900 in. (2,286 cm or 22.9 m) per minute. The feed rate in parts per minute is determined by dividing the linear feed rate per minute by the part length in the direction of feed, as shown in Figure 6-1. It should be noted that for very small parts, other factors become limiting and the general reference becomes invalid.

Vibratory Feed Systems

The most common bulk-feed system is a vibratory bowl, combined with gravity tracks, tubes, or "in-line" vibratory output tracks, as shown

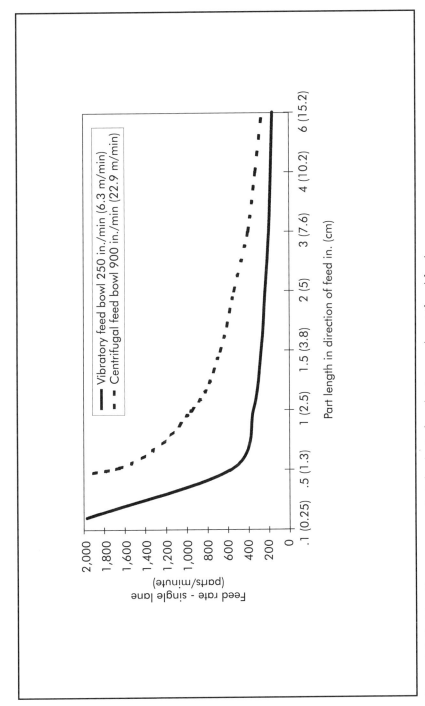

Figure 6-1. Part length versus upper limit feed rate for vibratory and centrifugal feeders.

in Figure 6-2. Most vibratory bowls are driven at 60 or 120 cycles per second (Hz) by simple, alternating-current coil drives. The oscillating (vibrating) motion of the bowl or linear feeder moves parts, lifts and pushes them forward, and returns before inertia allows the parts to fall and follow the tooling, as shown in Figure 6-3.

A vibratory system must be tuned. *Tuning* is the adjustment of the spring rates to match the bowl and part load inertia. Never overfill feed bowls. This "detunes" the bowl and reduces efficiency. Some manufacturers supply variable frequency drives that self-tune as the part load changes, or that can be set to run at a frequency that reduces noise or optimizes feed rate.

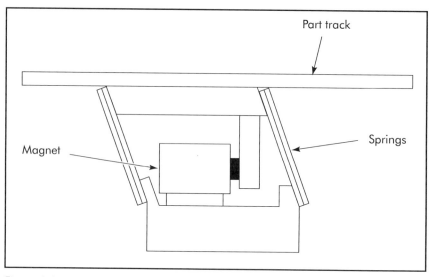

Figure 6-2. Linear vibratory feeder.

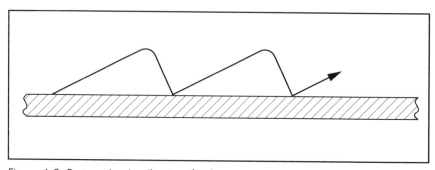

Figure 6-3. Part motion in vibratory feeder.

A helical track within the bowl moves parts up from the bottom, as shown in Figure 6-4. The track inside the bowl is usually wide enough to carry multiple parts for increased output. At the top of the helix, parts are oriented and selected by tooling. The tooling forces any incorrectly

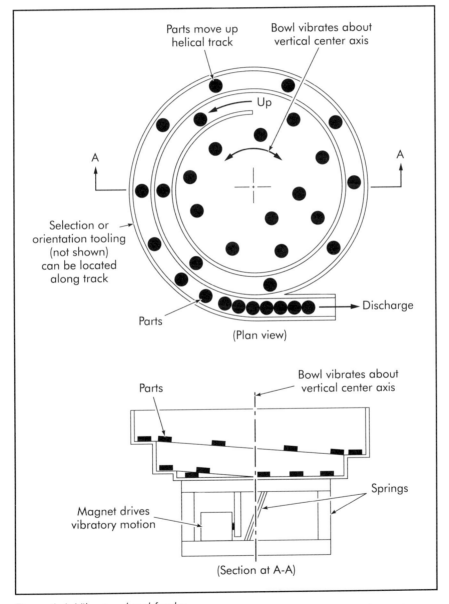

Figure 6-4. Vibratory bowl feeder.

oriented parts to return to the bowl or causes the part to be reoriented. This is usually done in stages, until only correctly oriented parts remain in the track. Many bowls cascade the feed track(s) down the outside of the bowl to continue the selecting process, allowing greater flexibility in tooling design. The use of air jets in the selection process is often necessary, but this practice should be discouraged due to the cost of compressed air, the noise, and dust it generates.

Vibratory feeders are very flexible and capable of feeding a wide variety of parts, for example, molded plastic parts; electrical components; glass vials; stamped, formed or machined parts; and many others.

For estimating purposes, assume that vibratory systems move parts at 4 in. (10.2 cm) per second (ips/cmps), although 6 ips (15.2 cmps) is possible. Output rate is then dependent on part length in output orientation, efficiency of the selection process, and losses due to lane balancing if multiple lanes are used. Thus, vibratory feeders can feed small parts at high rates, while larger parts are limited to lower rates.

Bowls can be designed to feed multiple lanes of parts. However, the efficiency per lane goes down as the number of lanes increases, because "good" lanes are limited to the output rate of the weakest lane (assuming the same output is required in each lane). Efficiency begins to drop significantly when more than three lanes are used.

Today, most feed bowls are constructed of stainless steel sheet metal. This offers good wear characteristics for most parts and allows the feeder supplier greater flexibility in designing and modifying the bowl. However, it also makes the feed bowl a great resonator, often creating unacceptable noise levels. It should be noted that tooling a vibratory bowl is not a science. A craftsman develops the tooling using experience and experimentation. Coatings, such as polyurethane, can be added to the bowl to protect delicate parts, modify friction characteristics, or reduce noise.

Most vibratory feed bowls require a sound enclosure. Any enclosure must allow easy operator access for loading parts, clearing jams, and performing routine maintenance on the feed system and other portions of the machine.

Centrifugal Feeders

Centrifugal bowl feeders are becoming increasingly common as speeds of assembly increase. They are typically used in bulk feed systems when a vibratory bowl can not feed enough parts to keep up with the assembly process.

A centrifugal bowl consists of two rotating members, one rotating within the other, as shown in Figure 6-5. The inner rotating member is usually a flat, or nearly flat, disk that may have ribs or other features to

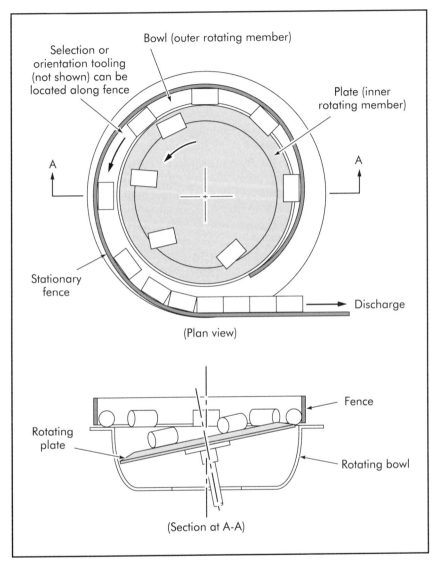

Figure 6-5. *Centrifugal bowl feeder.*

help it move the parts. This inner member rotates on an axis tilted slightly from vertical so that its surface tilts from horizontal. The outer member rotates around the inner, usually at a slightly higher speed and on a vertical axis. The outer member is a conical or spherical walled tub and its wall matches the inner member perimeter with minimal clearance. The outer member has a flat top ledge, approximately as wide as parts fed in their preferred orientation. An elevator system meters parts from a bulk hopper into a centrifugal bowl. Control of part quantity in the bowl is critical to the operation because too few, or too many, parts reduce the output. Parts drop from the elevator onto the inner rotating member, where they are accelerated to the member's peripheral speed. As parts accelerate, they move out to the edge of the inner member and up against the wall of the outer member. Inner member tilt is set to raise the parts up along the outer member wall and finally onto the flat top ledge. The ledge carries the parts through the orientation and selection tooling, and then to the output. Parts that make it onto the ledge incorrectly oriented are returned to the inner member by the selectors.

Orientation and selection tooling design can be passive or active and typically includes air jets. The member rotating speeds are adjusted to optimize feeding for both orientation and rate. Large bowls, up to 4 or 5 ft. (1.22 or 1.52 m) in diameter, typically rotate at 20-30 revolutions per minute (RPM), but they can be run at 40-50 RPM, if necessary. This gives a surface speed range of 50-150 in. (127-381 cm) per second at bowl perimeter (although small and special-purpose bowls can deviate significantly from this). This speed yields a theoretical output of up to 3,000 parts per minute for a 3-in. (7.6-cm) long part. However, the overall efficiency of the system is fairly low, and outputs are more typically in the range of 100 to 1,000 parts per minute.

The centrifugal bowl is a good choice for bulky, durable parts that need to be fed at high rates. Delicate or heavy parts also can be fed if bowl speeds are kept low. Typical centrifugal-fed parts include molded plastic parts; prepackaged parts; plastic bottles and caps; and stamped, formed, or machined metal parts. The highest feed rates generally correlate to parts with simple geometry, such as cylinders, disks, or blocks. Parts with complex geometry and subtle orientation features are difficult to feed with a centrifugal feeder.

Centrifugal bowls are quiet and durable, but the tooling and bowl surfaces are subject to wear from abrasive parts.

Since the short-term output of a centrifugal bowl can vary widely, there must be an accumulation system between the bowl and the assembly station. The output of a centrifugal bowl generally feeds into a high-speed conveyor system or into a gravity chute directly to an escapement. Conveyor types include air, flat belt, and flat-top chain. All of these can accumulate parts and create back pressure at the escapement if needed.

Elevating and Orienting Feeders

The elevating and orienting bulk feeder shown in Figure 6-6 depends on part shape or an asymmetrical center of gravity to cause incorrectly oriented parts to fall back into the hopper.

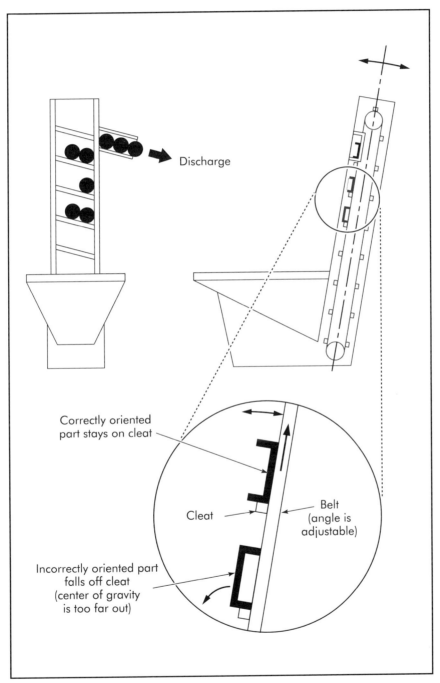

Figure 6-6. Elevating and orienting feeder.

Magazine Feed

Magazine-fed parts are handled in much the same manner as photographic slides in a projector (the older straight-line magazine style is more common in part handling). Magazines can be reusable or disposable. They are particularly useful for parts that can be damaged by bulk handling.

Magazine feeding systems can take some or all part orientation complications off-line, and they can be compact and quiet compared to bulk feeding systems.

Magazine feeding often follows one of the rules of good automation—orient and handle each part only once if possible. If parts can be loaded into magazines rather than bulk containers at the point of manufacture, this option should be pursued. Properly designed magazines protect parts from shipping damage and are often used primarily for that purpose. Thin parts, or those that stack easily, are ideal candidates for magazine feeding. Parts with holes can be loaded onto rods, which then function as a magazine. Parts that cannot be stacked, but must be carefully protected in shipping, are sometimes put into pocket trays. The tray can then be used as an input magazine for the assembly system. Electronic components are often handled in pocket trays.

The number of magazines, amount of floor space, and return/disposal are important considerations when designing for magazine-feed. Automatic magazine changing can reduce or eliminate downtime, but it can increase the cost of equipment.

Roll or Bandolier Feed

Label stock is an example of a roll-fed component: the component being a pressure-sensitive label attached to the base carrier. With roll feeding, a large number of parts can be supplied on one reel, minimizing downtime for changeovers. Roll feeding is also simple, low-cost, and has the capability to operate at high speeds.

Depending on the part or material, the difference in curvature between inner and outer wraps can change placement characteristics and the component itself. For example, label stock has more curl near the core and may feed differently. The diameter of the core should be determined based on performance at the dispensing station, as well as other factors. Small core diameters should be avoided because they increase feeding problems and add only a small percentage of parts.

When using roll-fed components that require precise placement, careful consideration must be given to the method of roll indexing and type of placement head.

There are many very useful variations on the basic roll-feed approach. One is to partially form the part and leave it attached to the carrier web for separation at final assembly. This is common in metal stamping, but also can be used with gaskets, thermoformed parts, and other components. Another is to attach parts to a separate carrier strip. Fasteners, such as nail strips for automatic nailers, are often handled in this manner.

A third variation of roll feeding is to place the part in a formed pocket on a carrier web. This is common in populating circuit boards with components fed from reels. Each component is in its own pocket and the parts are closely located. The pocket is covered by a strip that is removed just prior to assembly. The part is picked from the pocket by a robot or pick-and-place unit. Although this may seem like an elaborate part-feeding system, it is well established in circuit board manufacturing. This lends credibility to the earlier statement that part feeding is often the greatest challenge in automated assembly. Any method that improves the reliability of the final assembly equipment is worth investigating.

When winding on a core is not practical, consider using a bandolier feed system. A feed-strip of parts is layered zigzag fashion like a machine gun ammunition belt. If it is possible to access both ends of the bandolier, the next feed length can be spliced in while running. This eliminates downtime for roll changes, which is one of the primary drawbacks of core-wound feed systems.

Manufactured On-line

On-line manufacturing is the ultimate answer to eliminating handling and in-process inventory concerns. However, on-line manufacturing adds more complexity and can severely affect system reliability. As operations are tied together, upsets or jams in one operation affect all others and, therefore, the output of the total system. Refer to the discussion on "Accumulation (Buffers)" in Chapter 3.

Simple stamping is best done on-line. Springs that tangle can be wound on-line. Labels can sometimes be handled by on-line printing or laser etching. Injection molding can be integrated into an assembly line, but this requires careful evaluation of total system efficiency. Manufacturing on-line is the highest level of automated assembly and requires skill and experience to implement.

Flexible Feeding Systems

Flexible part feeding is an emerging technology generally applicable to low volumes, although high volumes can be achieved by using multiple systems. Flexible part feeding systems depend on a machine vision camera to view the site where the parts are located. The machine vision system analyzes the area to locate the correct part, determines its location and orientation, then determines if there is enough clearance around the part for the gripper to pick it up. The system conveys this information to the robot, which picks and places the part in the correct position in the product. Because of the amount of information programmed into the machine vision system, all parts necessary for a product can be placed in the site and the system can distinguish which one it needs first. By using an encoder, the system can track parts moving along on a conveyor and still pick up the correct part.

ESCAPEMENT

After parts are oriented and fed into a feed track, the next challenge is to separate them so that one, and only one, is escaped into the placement fixture or position. Although there are a few basic approaches, design of escapements is specific to the part being handled. Escapements can be a major source of jams and misfeeds if not designed well. Typical escapement designs are:

- Dead-end, pick out/push out;
- Coin change/shuttle/slide;
- Ratchet;
- Star wheel; and
- Feed screw.

Escapement and placement are often the most difficult operations to design and are frequently the reason for not using continuous motion.

As the speed of continuous-motion assembly increases, more consideration must be given to changes in the motion of the part, since the part starts at, or near, rest and must be accelerated to line speed in a very short time or distance. Under the best circumstances, part velocity should change very little and changes in direction should be gradual. The velocity and acceleration of a part moving through an assembly machine should be controlled by the design of the various feeds and transfers. Part motion should be controlled. With continuous-motion assembly equipment, extensive escapement prototyping is essential. Some techniques, such as the use of a star wheel and feed screw, are well suited to continuous motion. See Chapter 5 for more information on continuous-motion assembly.

Figure 6-7 shows some examples of escapements. Most of the escapements shown require a "choked feed" or a constant supply of parts with no gaps. Maintaining a choked feed, or instrumenting the system so that part or equipment damage does not occur if feed is interrupted, presents a significant challenge that must be addressed early in design.

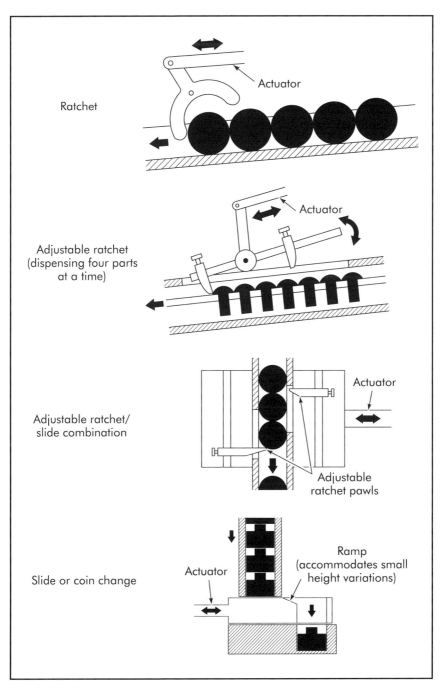

Figure 6-7. Escapements (Treer 1979).

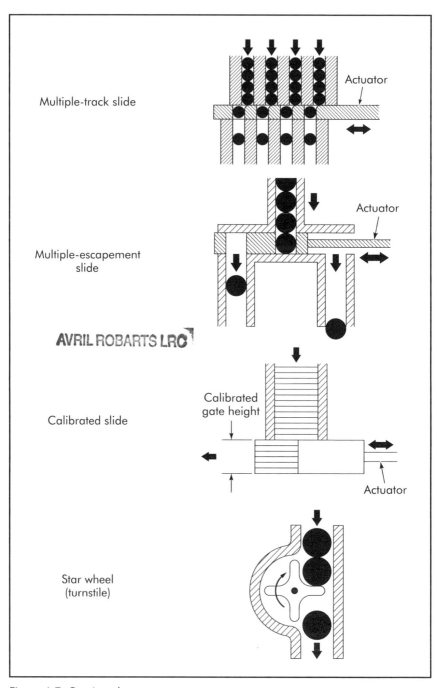

Multiple-track slide

Actuator

Multiple-escapement slide

Actuator

AVRIL ROBARTS LRC

Calibrated slide

Calibrated gate height

Actuator

Star wheel (turnstile)

Figure 6-7. Continued.

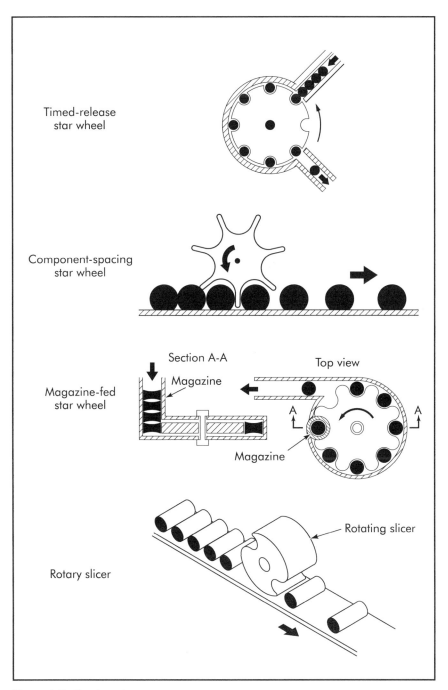

Figure 6-7. Continued.

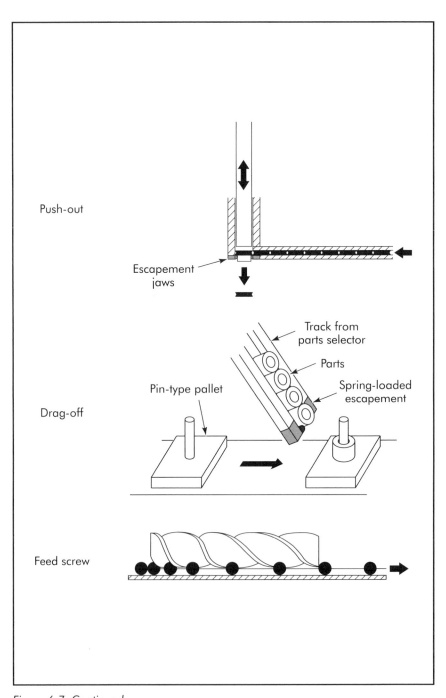

Push-out

Escapement
jaws

Track from
parts selector

Parts

Pin-type pallet

Spring-loaded
escapement

Drag-off

Feed screw

Figure 6-7. Continued.

SUMMARY

As assembly speeds increase, getting components to the right place, in the required orientation, and at the required rate often becomes the most difficult challenge in automating an assembly process. Understanding how each component is made is necessary to designing a reliable feed system. Component handling is not only important to the assembly operation; it impacts the entire manufacturing operation, including component suppliers.

Quality and consistency of components affects both the part-feeding operation and the reliability of the entire system.

REFERENCES

Boothroyd, Geoffrey. 1983. *Handbook of Feeding and Orienting Techniques for Small Parts*. Amherst, MA: University of Massachusetts, Department of Mechanical Engineering.

Treer, Kenneth R. 1979. *Automated Assembly* (Adaptation). Dearborn, MI: Society of Manufacturing Engineers.

7

Inspection and Measurement

INSPECTION: A CRITICAL COMPONENT

In general, it is good practice to inspect and verify each placement and process in an automated operation immediately after it is completed. If the inspection indicates a problem, succeeding operations can be bypassed. Most inspections can be accomplished using simple probes or other relatively straightforward techniques to determine if a part is in place and properly positioned. It is important to determine early in the design process what inspections are needed, since many inspections require an additional station. In addition to determining what inspections are needed, it also must be determined whether a go/no-go decision is sufficient or if a measurement is needed. Go/no-go decisions are simpler, but in many cases, measurement adds greatly to process understanding and process and product improvement.

Statistical process control (SPC) is a very important element in most production equipment today. Process information must be available to the operator for monitoring and control of the process. SPC, as well as inspection and measurement, are important topics, but are well documented in other sources and are, therefore, not covered in-depth here.

If an imperfect process operation can be detected by on-line inspection, it should be inspected. In cases where process control is relied upon to ensure quality, devote extra attention to developing the process, process parameters, and process control. If possible, process data from each product should be available to the control system and the operator for monitoring and process control charting.

Inspection of components prior to assembly is usually a more difficult task than inspecting operations during assembly. Incoming components can have a wide variety of defects and several inspection systems may be required to detect all possible flaws. In fact, some flaws may be impossible to detect automatically. However, after the assembly process has begun, the failure modes of each assembly step are more predictable and often can be inspected with simple devices. Refer to Chapter 8 for more information on the types of sensors available.

VISUAL INSPECTION AND MEASUREMENT

Some inspections are visual evaluations to determine whether an operation was completed correctly. Historically, operators have performed visual inspections. However, as speeds increase and inspection criteria become more complex, manual inspections become inadequate. Although human inspectors can interpret unusual situations, humans are inconsistent over time and make many errors. Studies show that humans make mistakes at a rate of about 6,000 errors per million actions, which is considered a four-sigma quality level (Motorola 7). This is true for airline baggage handlers, doctors writing prescriptions, restaurant cashiers, accountants making journal entries, and presumably, operators inspecting product quality. Very complex manual inspections have a much higher failure rate. In one example, circuit boards that were 100% visually inspected twice, using two different inspectors, had a product defect rate of 20% (200,000 defects per million) after inspection.

MACHINE VISION

Machine vision offers an excellent solution to many visual inspection problems. In the example cited earlier, when machine vision inspected the same circuit boards, defects dropped to six-sigma levels (approximately three defects per million) after inspection.

Machine vision is a very powerful, and rapidly advancing, technology that is just beginning to be exploited. It is being applied in nearly every industry, from medical to food products, and should be part of a company's automation plan. Successful application of machine vision requires a comprehensive understanding of process needs and a good understanding of machine vision technology. Unless the internal staff is skilled in this technology, outsourcing is probably the best alternative. Vision systems are most beneficial when used in a total system approach, designed into the manufacturing system from the start.

Note that the addition of a powerful and reliable machine vision inspection system often introduces unexpected results. A well-designed system usually finds more defects than anyone thought were being produced. *The addition of an automatic inspection system will usually cause an apparent increase in defects.* It is important to recognize that the actual number of defects has not changed, but that the system is now detecting more of them. A related factor is that human inspectors make subjective judgments, which can vary over time. An automatic inspection system makes decisions based on objective measurements and is very consistent over time. It is difficult to specify objective parameters for a vision system to match the more subjective judgment of a human.

Address this extremely important difference in advance by thoroughly discussing and documenting objective inspection criteria and resolving the subjective judgment issues. Even when this is done, further redefining of criteria is often necessary after the automated system is put on-line.

Many machine vision applications work in conjunction with automated manufacturing lines and robotics. Combining machine vision and robotics is referred to as *vision-aided robotics*. Machine vision greatly increases the robot's flexibility and decision-making capability and allows it to use randomly orientated parts. These systems are referred to as *flexible feed* systems and allow the robot to pick up a part in any orientation from point A and reorient the part in the correct position at point B. Parts at both locations can be moving.

Current circuit board assembly techniques employ vision-aided robotic technology. A *vision system* determines the precise location and orientation of the circuit board site and, using a second camera, determines the precise location of the component in the robot jaws. The robot compensates for any required correction. Placement of high-density surface-mount components uses "best-fit" algorithms to optimize results.

A machine vision system uses a charge-coupled device (CCD) array to capture an image of the object to be inspected. The image is composed of pixels—like those on a TV screen—that can be analyzed individually, or in groups, to make decisions about the object.

Since machine vision is a very specialized field, discuss specific applications with someone experienced in this area before assuming that a task can or cannot be done. Most applications can be tested and verified relatively easily on a commercial machine vision system. It is often possible to test the application on-line in the plant.

The following describes some machine vision fundamentals.

Fundamentals

Pixel   A picture element; the smallest sensing unit of a CCD (or similar type) camera.

Field-of-view (FOV)   The width or area imaged by a camera. Through lens selection, this could be the earth as viewed from a satellite or a tiny pin head viewed from a few millimeters.

Resolution   The "smallest" measurable unit a machine vision system can repeatedly attain. It is proportional to the FOV. For example, if a camera image contains 640 pixels while viewing the earth, which has a diameter of approximately 8,000 miles, the resolution is 8,000 miles/640 pixels = 12.5 miles per pixel. When viewing a pin with a 1/16 (.0625) in. diameter, the resolution is .0625 in./640 pixels = .0001 in. per pixel.

Gaging 10:1 rule   When using machine vision for gaging, the standard deviation (repeatability) of the gaging device should be ten times (10X) better than the tolerance on the item to be measured. For example, if part tolerance is ± .001, then the gage should be ± .0001. As low as six times (6X) can sometimes be allowed in extreme cases.

Lighting   This is the most critical aspect of machine vision. Lighting must provide constant illumination of the object to be imaged by the camera. Techniques used include backlighting, front lighting, diffusion, focused, and collimated. Machine vision experts attribute 80% to 90% of the success of an application to lighting.

Structured lighting   Structured lighting refers to specific light patterns used to illuminate an object, such as a series of laser generated lines. Structured lighting, most notably laser generated patterns, can provide three-dimensional data using standard inspection systems, as shown in Figure 7-1. The light pattern is projected at an angle and any change in the elevation of the surface causes an offset as viewed by the camera. The vision system uses the offset to calculate the relative height of the surface.

Speed   A relative measurement of the time required to take a picture, process the data, and display or send the results to the real world. Current machine vision systems can typically do this at rates faster than five inspections per second.

1D line scan   A type of camera that takes a single line of picture data at a time. These cameras are generally used in high-resolution applications where surface speed is greater than 150 ft (45.7 m) per minute. Line-by-line processing is becoming more prevalent with the growth of line-by-line gathering and assembly into a two-dimensional image for processing. For example, it is used for web inspection and surface flaw detection.

2D area array   A type of camera that uses an area scene looking at two-dimensional objects. Standard television output is an example. These cameras are generally used in moderate-resolution applications for inspection of objects or patterns. Object speed is usually limited to 150 ft (45.7 m) per minute. For example, it is used for circuit boards, piece parts, and printed webs.

REJECT SYSTEMS

After a defect or error is detected in the part, it must be prevented from mixing with the good ones. When the assembly is captured in tooling, rejecting the correct unit can be done reliably. When the assembly is not positively located, reliably rejecting the flawed unit and not re-

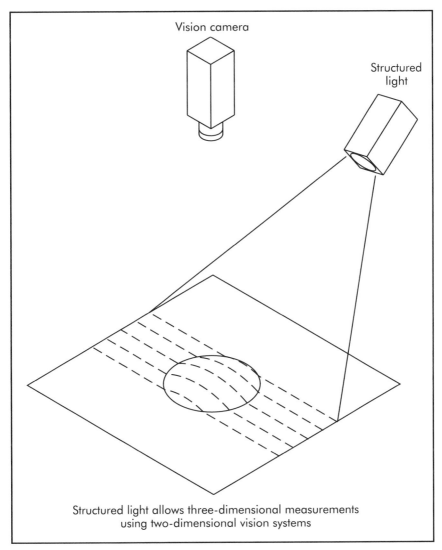

Figure 7-1. Structured lighting.

jecting adjacent good product can be difficult, especially if high speeds are involved. Reaction time from flaw detection to reject system actuation becomes an issue at high speeds. Physical movement of the reject device can be difficult to time correctly, since an electric solenoid or air cylinder often accomplishes it. Timing can be set during steady-state running. However, the reject system must work reliably during all machine conditions. The importance of the basic premise, "never lose control of a part," is evident.

Consider the reliability of removing flawed product, data reporting of flaws by cause, and whether all rejects should be put in one container or separated by flaw. For example, repairable flaws can be separated from others to eliminate sorting later.

SUMMARY

Inspection and measurement are vital to the success of any automated assembly operation. Determine what inspections and measurements are necessary early and plan for them in equipment design. Although go/no-go inspections are often adequate, consider making actual measurements, since the additional information can be very useful in process understanding and improvement.

Machine vision is a particularly powerful technology, but requires more physical space and more planning than other methods. Inspection must be done while the part or product is under control to ensure that inspection data can be attributed to a specific product and that the correct product is rejected.

REFERENCE

"Integrating the Quality Process within the Business Process." Undated monograph. Schaumburg, IL: Motorola, Inc.: 7.

Control Systems

DEFINITION

The control system of an automated assembly machine is the electrical, electronic, pneumatic, and mechanical system that monitors and coordinates the operation of the machine. The control system may be as simple as a motor spinning a shaft with a couple of cams that control the mechanisms, or, it could be a large and complex system with many processors coordinating hundreds of sensors and dozens of motors. All but the smallest machines need a control strategy, sensors, one or more controllers, an operator interface, actuators, and information management.

DESIGN

Every control system should be designed to be dependable and maintainable. Future production needs should be considered so that the assembly machine may be modified over its lifetime to adapt to changes in the product or process. The control system hardware and software should be clearly and completely documented. Mechanical systems can usually be understood by observation. However, control systems usually cannot be readily understood by observation and, therefore, require thorough documentation.

The design of the control system involves many considerations and decisions during the initial design phase. They are:

- Which operations should be automated, and which should be done by an operator?
- Which operations should be mechanically linked, and which should be electronically linked and controlled?
- What actuators should be used?
- What operations, processes, and parts should be sensed?
- When and how should the parts be tested?
- Should the control be centralized in one controller or distributed over many processors?
- How should the assembly machine communicate with the other machines and conveyors it receives parts from or supplies parts to?

- How will the machine communicate process information to the manufacturing information system (MIS)?
- What will be required of the machine in the future and how can the control system be designed to accommodate anticipated upgrades?

The initial control system design work is accomplished through the answering of these questions. The next steps involve the more detailed work of choosing specific sensors, actuators, and controllers. A control system layout diagram can then be drawn and the controller software can be written.

MACHINE CONTROLLERS

Machine controllers are specially designed computers that are optimized for industrial machine control. They are used to implement all of the machine logic, control, and data gathering and communicate machine and process information to other machines and plant information systems. Most assembly machines require at least one controller; some may need a dozen or more.

The following are the types of controllers commonly used in assembly machines.

- *Programmable logic controllers* (PLCs) execute all of the machine discrete logic and coordinate the operation of other machine controllers. PLCs are used as the primary controller in most production equipment, including assembly machines.
- *Motion controllers* control the speed, position, and torque of any direct current (DC), brushless, or stepper motors. The controllers vary widely in the style of hardware and software design. They are usually programmed using a language developed by the controller manufacturer and many offer programming in a standard language.
- *Personal computer (PC) -based process controllers* are gradually replacing PLCs for logic control. The use of PCs for machine control will increase with the development of real-time program applications. When compared to PLCs, PCs offer advantages that include a standard hardware and operating system, and seamless connection to many software applications.
- *Proportional integral derivative (PID) loop controllers* maintain temperature, pressure, flow, and other linear processes. Most of these controllers have a few parameters that are configured; some can run simple programs that control a process through a series of states.
- Specific purpose controllers, such as machine vision, robots, bar code readers, and other types of sensors and actuators are often on

proprietary hardware platforms. The use of PCs to control these systems is increasing as PCs become more powerful.

- Embedded electronic controllers are designed to perform a specific task. These are economical when many identical machines will be built.

The size and complexity of the machine, the degree of automation, and the number and types of sensors and actuators all contribute to the controller requirements. Most assembly machines need, at minimum, a PLC to control the discrete on/off machine operations. Many machines also need motion controllers, and some require PID or other dedicated controllers.

Computers used as machine controllers should perform all tasks in a well-defined and consistent manner. Their responsibilities are generally limited to monitoring inputs and updating the state of outputs (input/output or I/O), executing the control program, communicating with other computers, and monitoring internal operations. These operations are guaranteed to always occur within a specific time, so that the control system designer can predict how fast the controller will react to changing machine conditions. Machine controllers execute application software written in various machine controller languages, which are optimized for speed and functionality.

The high machine speeds of many assembly machines put some unique demands on the machine controllers. Processing speed and I/O update rates become critical when the production rates exceed 50 parts per minute, which is one part every 20 milliseconds (msec). The assembly of each part is made up of a few steps that share the time allowed for the part, and the processor has to control the steps sequentially. The time to perform some tasks may be a few msec, and in some situations, the controller may have to respond to an input in less than one msec. Many machine, motion, and process controllers are not able to operate at these speeds and, therefore, are unsuitable for the control of high-speed assembly equipment. *The controllers chosen must have I/O update times and program execution times at least twice as fast as the fastest response needed to a change in an input.* Typical PLC program execution times are in the tens of milliseconds range, and many servo motion controllers have servo loop execution times as fast as 40 msec.

The choice of which controller(s) to use is an important one and should be decided only after clearly defining the system requirements and evaluating the many options. The controller choice determines the control system capabilities, personnel training requirements, expansion capability, communication network capability, and control system configuration. Following are some issues that must be considered when choosing controllers.

- Will control be distributed or centralized? Distributed control uses many small controllers to perform specific control tasks at a machine subsection. Centralized control uses one large controller to perform all tasks.
- If control is distributed, how will it be coordinated? Distributed control can be coordinated through a master/slave organization or a network of peers.
- What are the future machine control needs? There must be a clearly defined migration path for controller upgrades.
- What are the controller communication requirements?
  - Bus-based controllers or networked controllers;
  - Control network or information handling network; and
  - Communication speed and protocol.
- What are the network requirements? Multiple networks are often used. I/O modules usually have a dedicated network, while controllers and operator panels often share a network. Since the plant will have some type of process data gathering network, the controller responsible for collecting machine data should connect with it.
- What level of plant maintenance support is available? Controllers execute application programs written by systems engineers. Plant maintenance personnel need to be trained to understand the controller and software to troubleshoot the system when there are machine breakdowns.
- What level of vendor support is available? The controller manufacturer and distributor need to be readily available to help the plant with any problems that maintenance cannot solve.

In general, controllers should be selected to accomplish the tasks needed. The control system should be kept as simple as possible, and there should be a planned migration path to any likely machine expansion. They need to be supported in the plant, so the plant must be committed to training enough people to work with them. All controllers should have a communication link to the other controllers on the assembly machine so that they can share information about the machine. In addition, the machine control system should communicate to the other machines in the process and have a communication link to the plant process data information system.

The machine controllers for a typical large assembly machine utilizing a distributed control strategy are shown in Figure 8-1. The control of the machine is distributed between three PLCs with digital and analog I/O, two servo drive controllers, a vision system, two CRT operator

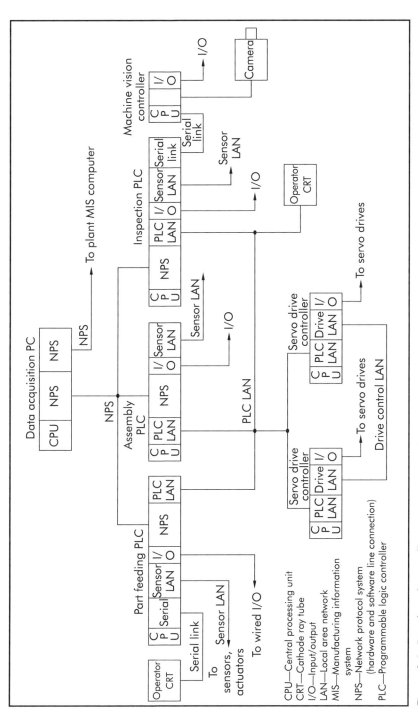

Figure 8-1. Distributed controller communication diagram.

CPU—Central processing unit
CRT—Cathode ray tube
I/O—Input/output
LAN—Local area network
MIS—Manufacturing information
   system
NPS—Network protocol system
   (hardware and software line connection)
PLC—Programmable logic controller

control panels, and a PC. The assembly operation in this example is made up of three sections: one section that feeds parts; one that assembles the parts; and a third section that inspects the parts, rejects the parts that fail inspection, and moves the acceptable parts to the next machine.

Each of the three sections is controlled by a separate PLC. This allows the machine sections to be built, debugged, and run independent of the other sections, an important feature during debug, checkout, and troubleshooting. Each servo drive controller controls one to eight servo motors that move and position the parts and machine tooling to perform the assembly operations. The vision inspection system measures the quality of the final product and accepts or rejects each part based upon programmed parameters. One of the operator CRTs is used to control only the part feeding section, while the second CRT is connected to all three PLCs and is used to coordinate the control of all three machine sections. The PC is used to gather data from all of the controllers, process the data into information that is useful, display the information at the machine, and communicate the information to the plant management information system (MIS). It also may be used to direct what products are to be manufactured, along with any other machine setup parameters that may be needed.

The controllers are connected to each other over local area networks (LANs), which are serial data communication links that allow information to be passed between the controllers. The three PLCs, the two servo drive controllers, and one of the cathode ray tubes (CRT) are connected over a supervisory PLC-LAN that is used to integrate the operation of the three machine sections. Information passed over this network is of two types: instructions to the controllers coming from the PC and the operator CRT, and information about the process sent from the controllers to the other controllers, the PC, and the operator CRT. Instructions to the controllers include directions about which part is to be assembled, machine operation instructions, and run state. The controllers communicate their status, including process variable information and any fault conditions. Real-time control information is not sent out on this LAN because it cannot be moved between the controllers fast enough to control the assembly process.

The PLCs communicate to the PC over a high-speed PC network connection LAN. Providing a separate LAN for monitoring PLC I/O increases the throughput of I/O data and keeps the PC communications from slowing down information moving across the PLC-LAN.

The servo drive controllers use a high-speed control LAN to coordinate the motion of the servo motors. These LANs are suitable for many real-time control instructions between controllers, but some control functions need to be executed faster than the LAN will allow. For example, a motor in one controller may be electronically geared to follow a motor speed and position controlled by the other controller. The LAN may not be able to communicate the motor positions fast enough for the following motor to accurately keep up. In these instances, the necessary signals, like motor position feedback, must be wired separately to each controller that needs the information.

In Figure 8-1, the vision controller is shown connected to the inspection PLC over a serial link. This is only one of many possible configurations. In this example, the communication is slow and the information is limited to the product being run and a count of good and bad products. The vision controller is given the responsibility of controlling the mechanisms that accept and reject the parts after inspection.

A sensor LAN is used to connect sensors and motor drives to the part-feeding PLC. The devices that can communicate on this LAN are intelligent sensors and actuators that often can be configured to perform some minimal control tasks. Most devices provide some degree of self diagnostics. Using intelligent devices on a sensor LAN distributes responsibility for control to the lowest level. Even if the control is not executed at the sensor LAN device, using these intelligent devices on a sensor LAN is recommended. The diagnostic capabilities of the devices and the simplified wiring makes the control system more reliable.

SOFTWARE

The controller software is a critical part of the control system. This software resides in the PLC, the PC, the motion controller, and any of the other processors that may be used to control the assembly machine. It implements all of the control system algorithms and discrete logic needed to control the machine. The software processes all of the machine and process data, and makes it available for the operators, process engineers, and the plant operations database.

To provide the most useful machines, the following features should be offered in the control system software.

- The software should be written in a structured manner, with the machine operations organized around logical machine states. The machine is then always in a defined state until it completes the actions associated with that state and is allowed to move on to the next state or states. The traditional way to accomplish this is with a main program made up of program calls to subroutines that perform various machine operations. Now, with PLC and PC controller manufacturers supporting an international standard for PLC control languages, the program can be organized with a real state language. Writing the code in a state language makes the program faster to write, simpler to understand, easier to modify, and easier for plant maintenance to support in the field.

- The software must contain diagnostic code that detects any likely machine problem. The software directs the operation of the machine to a safe condition, alerts the operator of the problem, and explains to the operator what the proper fault-correction procedure is, so that machine downtime is kept to a minimum.
- Starting and stopping the machine are often the most difficult procedures to program. For the program to start the machine properly under all circumstances, it is necessary to define the various initial conditions that may be present at startup. Since the machine may fault or be stopped at any time during its cycle, the software must be able to stop the machine smoothly and move it to an initial start-up condition. Many machines accomplish this with a "Reset Mode" that moves all mechanisms to an initial position, where they are ready to start a new cycle.
- All assembly machines should have a "Manual and/or Maintenance Mode" that allows the machine actuators to be run independently. This makes it much easier for maintenance to troubleshoot the equipment and make machine adjustments. It may even be worth the effort to write a program that cycles parts of the machine or operates the machine in slow motion.

The plant process engineering and maintenance departments must provide the software maintenance necessary to keep the machine operating for its entire life cycle. Therefore, some plant maintenance personnel need to be trained to use the controllers and the software.

There should be established procedures for maintaining the backup storage media that contain the control system software. Only authorized personnel—following the established procedures—should be allowed to make and document software changes. If the software controlling the production machinery is different from that on the backup file held by maintenance, the machine cannot be brought back to its current operating state after a processor failure.

SENSORS

Sensors are a very important and integral component in the field of automation. They are the foundation on which the control system makes its decisions. Since sensors provide a wide range of process information, there are many sensor types from which to choose.

With the wide variety of materials that need to be sensed, there is some overlapping of sensor applications. For example, a sensor type typically used for process control also might be used in an automated assembly system.

Because the focus here is on automated assembly engineering rather than process control engineering, this review does not cover thermocouples, pressure gages, flow meters, and related sensor types. Instead, this chapter will concentrate on sensors used primarily for controlling automated assembly machines. These types of *sensors* provide information related to the presence, position, and velocity of production parts and machine actuators.

Each automated assembly machine design has specific sensor requirements related to process control. These requirements are dependent on many factors, such as physical size constraints, response time, type of material being sensed, electrical interface requirements, reliability, resolution, cost, and the environment in which it will be used.

Sensors used with automated assembly systems include, but are not limited to, the following:

- Bar code systems;
- Encoders and resolvers;
- Height gages;
- Laser sensors;
- Magnetostrictive sensors;
- Mechanical switches;
- Photoelectric sensors;
- Proximity sensors;
- Sensor networks; and
- Vision systems.

Photoelectric Sensors

Photoelectric sensors are one of the most commonly used sensor types for automated assembly systems. This is due, in part, to fiber optic technology and the design flexibility it offers. There are two types of fiber optic assemblies: individual and bifurcated, as shown in Figure 8-2.

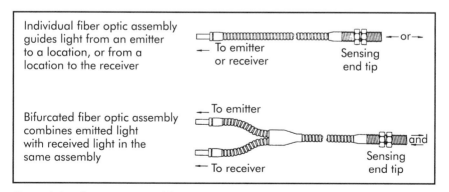

Figure 8-2. Fiber optic assemblies.

Photoelectric Sensing Modes

Although the sensing requirements of an application may be satisfied in many ways, usually one sensing mode is best suited to the situation. The sensing modes most often used with automated assembly machines are shown in Figure 8-3.

Proximity Sensors

Proximity sensors are used to detect objects that come within a set distance of the sensor. This distance varies with the type of sensor, its sensitivity, and the type of material sensed. There are three basic types of proximity sensors: inductive, capacitive, and ultrasonic. Some popular applications for proximity sensors are shown in Figure 8-4.

An inductive proximity sensor is typically used for sensing conductive materials, such as steel, stainless steel, lead, brass, aluminum, copper, and other metals.

A capacitive sensor can be used for sensing both conductive and non-conductive materials. Because of this feature, it is usually used to sense liquid or product fill levels, or product presence within a container. It is also two to three times more expensive than an inductive sensor.

The ultrasonic type is not used as often as other sensors because it is expensive, and most applications can be accommodated by an inductive or capacitive sensor. An ultrasonic sensor costs four to five times more than an inductive sensor. It is used when the sensor cannot be close to the object to be sensed. Ultrasonic sensors can detect objects at distances of a few yards.

Vision Systems

The capability most needed in the automated assembly field is the ability to sense the presence, position, and orientation of very complicated parts. Vision systems offer a wide variety of tools for use in automated assembly applications. They can be used very effectively for process control. Vision systems are discussed in detail in Chapter 7. Laser and photocell arrays can sometimes be used as a simpler alternative to a vision system.

Magnetostrictive Sensors

Figure 8-5 shows magnetostrictive sensors that are used to determine linear position. They are a popular replacement for linear potentiometers, with a wear life expectancy 50 times greater. Typical sensing lengths are from 3-48 in. (8-122 cm). Accuracy is ±.05% with full-stroke repeatability of .01%. Though linear potentiometers are still popular, magnetostrictive sensing is becoming very cost competitive—especially when considering wear life expectancy and accuracy.

Retroflective mode
The sensor contains both an emitter and a receiver. A light beam is bounced off a retroflective target and an object is sensed when it interrupts the beam. It is good for applications that allow scanning from one side only. However, this mode may not detect an object with a highly reflective surface.

Diffuse mode
Like a reflective mode sensor, this sensor also contains an emitter and a receiver. In this case, however, the object to be detected is the reflective target. When light strikes the object, a small percentage of the diffused light is reflected back to the receiver. This mode is well suited for applications that require sensing objects with reflective surfaces.

Opposed mode
With this mode, the emitter and receiver are positioned opposite each other, with the beam shining directly at the receiver. An object is detected when it breaks the beam. This is the most efficient sensing mode, requiring the least amount of optical energy. It is also the most reliable mode when the object to be detected is opaque and does not allow light to pass through it.

Apertured mode
This mode functions in the same manner as the opposed mode. However, the lenses are apertured to limit the field of view. This mode is useful for detecting small parts, inspecting small profiles, and sensing position accurately.

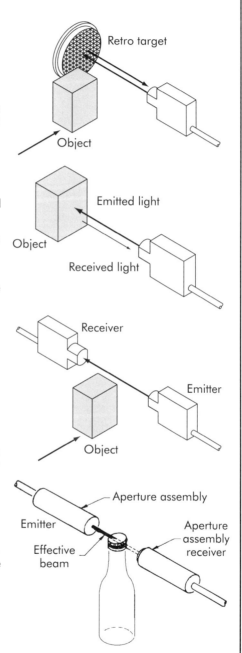

Figure 8-3. Photoelectric sensing modes.

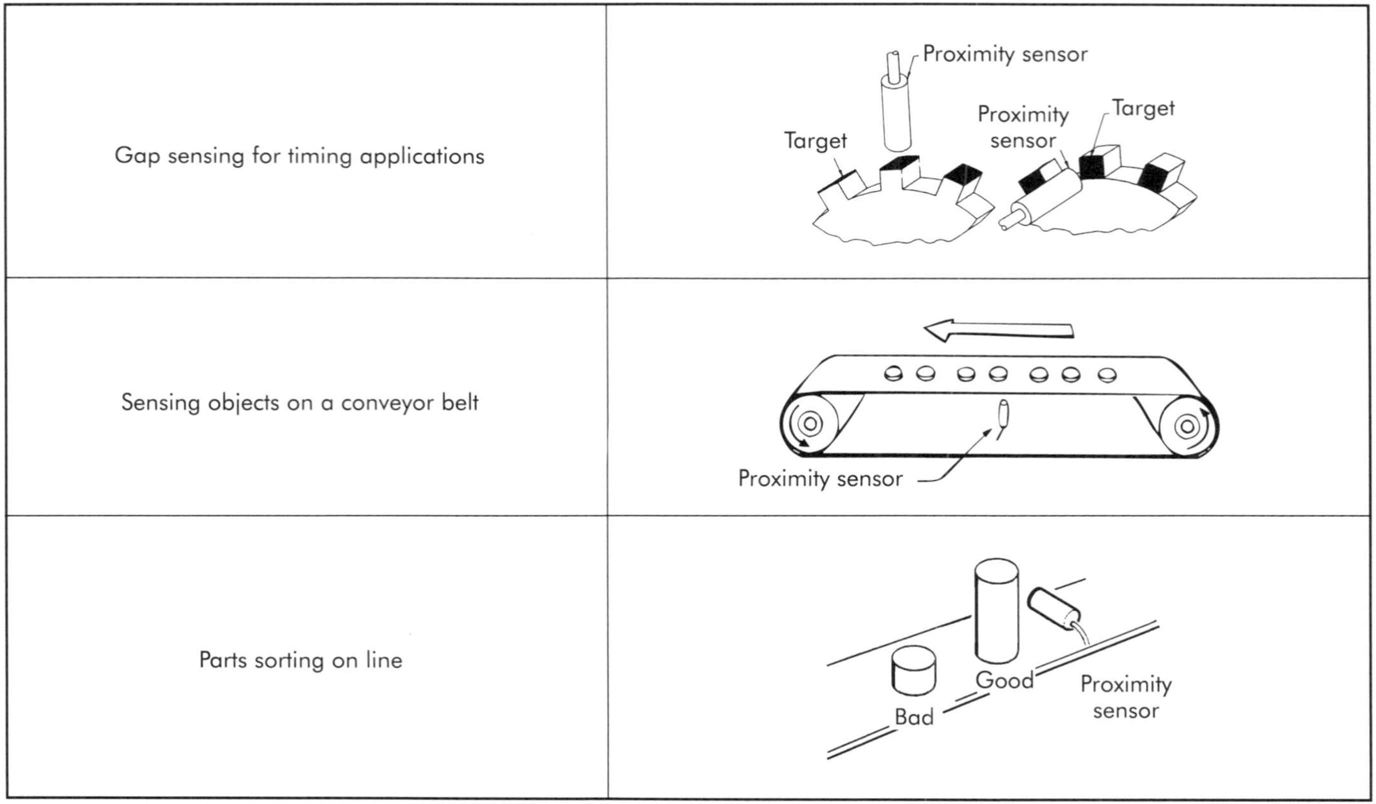
Gap sensing for timing applications
Proximity sensor
Target
Proximity sensor
Target
Sensing objects on a conveyor belt
Proximity sensor
Parts sorting on line
Good
Bad
Proximity sensor

Figure 8-4. Proximity sensor applications.

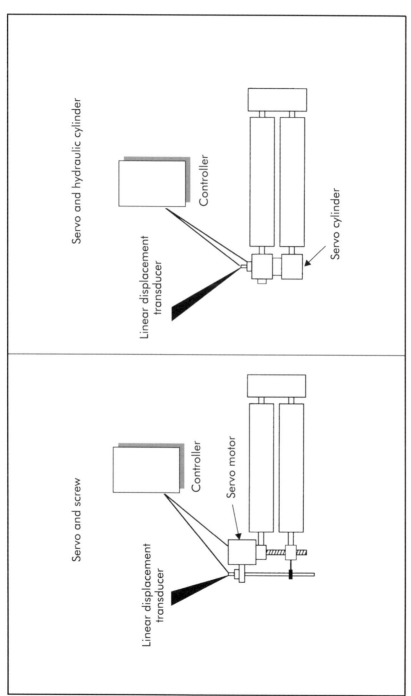

Figure 8-5. Two magnetostrictive solutions for roller gap control.

Bar Code Systems

Bar code systems are a very common technology. Most people have seen a universal product code (U.P.C.) label on any number of consumer products. This code is scanned by a bar code reader, usually at a checkout counter, and the scanned information is compared with a database. The system then returns information, such as the price, to the electronic cash register. Bar code systems are also used to electronically inventory products.

Automated assembly bar code systems function in basically the same manner as retail store bar code systems. For example, U.P.C. labels are attached to pallets that transport products from station to station during assembly. The U.P.C. label is scanned at each workstation, and the scanned information is used to update the database. The database contains all the information each station requires to perform its function, including pass/fail data, worker assignments, build schedules, and other system control information. Bar code systems also allow a database to be built with all the important process and raw material information for each part.

Automated part retrieval systems use bar code data to control pallet movement. The central computer initiates action by requesting a particular pallet to move to a designated location. The pallet handling equipment then reads the pallet bar codes, selects the proper pallet, and verifies the selection with the central computer. In this manner, the bar code system provides the feedback information required by the central computer to close the control loop.

Encoders and Resolvers

Encoders are generally rotary devices, but linear encoders are also used. There are basically two encoder types: incremental and absolute.

Incremental encoders provide a continuous train of pulses that can be used to determine speed and position, provided there is a known point of reference. They are used most often for accurate positioning of mechanical arms, belts, or pulleys. However, they can also provide speed and position feedback to the drive for performance control. Position information can be used in a manner similar to a cam to trigger various sequential actions.

Absolute encoders, though similar, provide users with the actual position at all times, which enables the system to calculate speed as well. They eliminate the need for a homing sequence after power-up. Absolute encoders are often specified for applications where the position of a mechanical arm or component in a nested position on a belt must be known at power-up to prevent damage or eliminate a complicated homing sequence. They should be used to keep track of a rotary machine's position, so the controller can use machine position to monitor and control the machine.

Encoders come in a large range of resolutions, with higher resolution encoders being more expensive. One of the main encoder components is an etched glass disk, which must be protected from damage. Do not use a hammer or drop an encoder during the installation, and do not use it in an application where it is exposed to excessive physical contact.

A resolver is a good alternative to use instead of an encoder when ruggedness is needed. A *resolver* is an analog device with three windings, very similar to a generator. The rotor winding is attached to the shaft where the position is to be measured. This winding is excited with a high-frequency signal. This signal creates a magnetic field that induces a sine wave and a cosine wave in the two stator windings. These two signals are dependent on the rotor position. Electronics are used to decode the sine and cosine signals to determine rotor position. Resolvers are more expensive than encoders and are not able to resolve rotary position into as many discrete positions as encoders. Resolvers are mainly used for servo motor speed and position feedback.

Mechanical Switches

Prior to the tremendous advances in sensor technology, mechanical switches were used quite extensively in control applications. Due to improved reliability and performance, mechanical switches are still used regularly for this purpose—but primarily in locations where switch actuation and wear are minimized to increase life expectancy. Although there are many types of switches available, mechanical switches are used more often than others for controlling an automated assembly process. An extensive choice of actuator profiles enables limit switches to be specified for a wide variety of applications.

Height Gages

Height gages are devices that measure distance based on the amount of physical displacement, similar to a caliper. They utilize capacitive pulsing, optical linear encoder, linear variable differential transformer, and even laser encoder principles to determine the displacement. Measurement resolution accuracy is typically .0005 - .00005 in. (0.0127-.00127 mm), depending on the type of height gage.

Height gages are used in automated assembly and process control applications to measure the height or thickness of a part, and occasionally to indicate the presence of a part. In some instances, it is necessary to perform both functions. When parts are stacked on an assembly, measuring height may be a very convenient way to detect part presence.

Height gages also may be employed in tandem to measure the presence of a small or thin component added to an assembly. One gage would serve as a reference, and the other would measure the component.

Laser Sensors

Laser sensors are high-precision sensors that can be used in displacement, through-beam, or scanner applications. They offer the following advantages:

- Depending on the sensor and application, the operating range can be from .01-12 in. (0.25-304.8 mm);
- Measuring accuracy down to .00008 in. (0.002 mm);
- Repeatability to .00001 in. (0.00025 mm); and
- Response times down to 0.15 ms (6.6 kHz [Hz = cycles per second]).

Laser sensors are used in a broad range of detecting, measuring, and positioning applications, as shown in Figure 8-6.

Sensor Networks

Networking technology is being applied in numerous office and industrial applications to connect many users or data acquisitions terminals. The key to successful networking is the communication structure. A wide choice of structures offers an opportunity to minimize the number of data lines or communication cables required to interconnect all systems. This, in turn, can significantly reduce installation costs.

Networking technology is also being applied to sensors, which are generally field-mounted devices. Normally, all wires from field-mounted sensors must be routed back to control panels. This can require many lengths of wire and extensive labor. With sensors designed for network use, a single cable is routed from sensor to sensor, minimizing wire and labor costs.

Networked sensors are intelligent sensors that are able to do more than convert a process variable into an electrical signal. These smart sensors are often able to report internal faults and the degradation of the measured signal, and to accept recalibration by the controller. Some can be programmed to perform simple control tasks, such as turning on an output whenever it senses an object. Intelligent sensors linked to a controller over a serial network offer some important advantages over the traditional analog sensors and should be used whenever practical.

OPERATOR CONTROL PANELS

The *control panel* is a window into an assembly machine that operators, process engineers, and maintenance personnel use to control machine operations and to extract machine and process information. A control panel should provide all the information and controls needed to

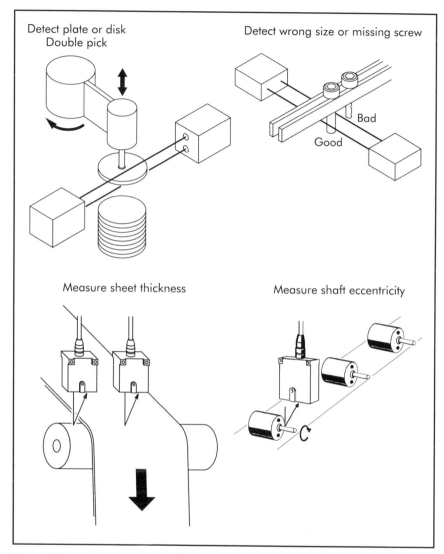

Figure 8-6. Laser sensor applications.

operate the machine. The information should be presented in a manner that is easily understood, and control should be simple and straightforward. Alarms and machine diagnostics should be included, and future expansion needs should be considered.

Most operator control panels incorporate a programmable screen and keypad. The advantages of a programmable display when compared to

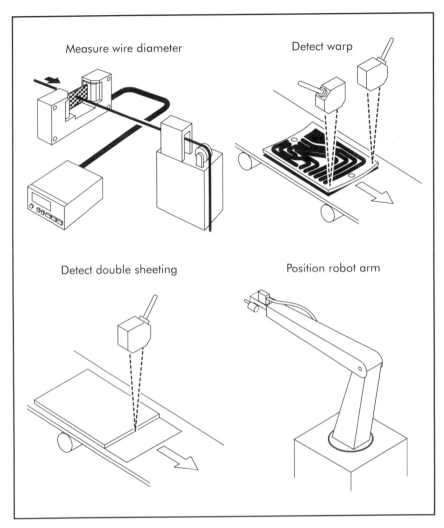

Measure wire diameter

Detect warp

Detect double sheeting

Position robot arm

Figure 8-6. Continued.

hard-wired controls include cost, compactness, flexibility for changes and expansion, the ability to reside on a network with access to information from many processors, excellent alarming and troubleshooting tools, process data display capabilities, and historical trending capabilities. The cost of programmable displays has been reduced to the point where they are now cost effective when replacing as few as six push buttons and two meters. This makes them practical for use on small assembly machines. There are two main types of programmable operator control panels.

1. Liquid crystal display (LCD) or CRT configurable terminals with touch screen or membrane keypads; and
2. PCs running an operator interface and/or process control software.

LCD or CRT configurable terminals are the most common. They communicate with the machine controllers over a serial link or a PLC-LAN, and display information sent from the controllers.

A PC-based system should be considered when there is a requirement for many control loops, process variable display and trending, specialized PC controllers (such as vision inspection systems), or additional PC-based software (such as statistical process control). Configurable terminals are often used in conjunction with PC-based control panels. If there is no requirement for PC-based operator control, a configurable terminal is recommended.

All operator control panels should clearly indicate all machine faults. The cause of the problem, such as part jam, out of parts, dropped part, mechanism jam, motor overcurrent, or measured variable out of range, must be indicated. The action that the operator must take in each instance also should be indicated. If the problem requires maintenance action, instructions to maintenance personnel on how to fix the problem should be displayed on a CRT or available in the machine maintenance manual.

MOTION CONTROL

The precise control of mechanical motion is very important in automated assembly machines. Any work that is performed on a part requires motion control to bring the part into the machine, perform the work, and move the part out of the machine.

Motion control directs the position, speed, torque, and force of a part or device. Control can be open or closed loop; it can range from crude to very precise; and it can vary widely in response time. There may be no feedback, or there could be speed, position, and torque feedback. The most common actuators used to control motion are motors, pneumatic cylinders, and solenoids. Cam and drive shafts are common transmission elements used to move and position parts and tooling.

Motors are the most versatile motion control device because of the wide range of speeds, sizes, and motor types available. The most common types of motors used in assembly equipment are: AC induction, DC, brushless AC, and stepper motors.

AC Induction Motors

AC induction motors are the most widely used motors. They are designed to run at a constant speed, which is determined by the winding design and the frequency of the voltage. A constant-speed AC motor is used for pumps, fans, conveyors, and mixers. A gear box is often used to set the shaft speed and torque. The stator is the armature, and the field is induced in the rotor by the rotating magnetic field created in the stator.

Speed control of an AC motor is possible using a variable frequency drive (VFD). This is often a good solution for a motion control application that needs a speed range of less than 5 to 1, speed regulation of no better than 5%, and power requirements that are in the fractional to integral horsepower range.

DC Motors

DC motors with brush commutation have been used traditionally for accurate speed control and when high torque or horsepower (into the hundreds) is required. They are generally not used for motion control.

With DC motors, the rotor is the armature and the current is mechanically commutated through two brushes. Speed regulation is as good as the speed feedback allows—better than 1% regulation is common when using a high-quality tachometer or an encoder.

Although DC motors are a bit cheaper and simpler than brushless motors, they require brush and commutator maintenance. However, a case can be made for them when cost is more critical than performance.

Brushless AC Motors

Brushless AC motors have eliminated brush-type DC motors from many applications. Brushless AC motors, like an AC induction motor, have a three-phase armature in the stator. The rotor has permanent magnets, which causes it to follow the rotating magnetic field circulating around it. The armature is electronically commutated, using rotor position feedback, usually with Hall-effect sensors to detect rotor position. Speed and position control are accomplished by using feedback from a rotor-mounted encoder or resolver.

Brushless AC motors have many advantages over DC brush motors.

- The armature current is in the stator instead of the rotor. Heat created by the armature current is dissipated more effectively than it is in a brush motor that runs the armature current through the rotor.
- Brushless AC motors can handle more current and, therefore, create more torque than a DC brush motor of the same size.
- Because the rotor has magnets instead of current-carrying conductors, an AC motor is smaller and lighter than a DC motor.
- The rotor has less inertia, so it can accelerate and decelerate faster than a comparable DC motor.

Because of their many advantages, brushless AC motors are normally used for speed and position control. However, a DC brush motor may be used if the life of the machine is short enough so that long-term maintenance will not be an issue, or when a large horsepower motor is needed and a brushless motor is not available.

The disadvantages of a brushless AC motor are the higher purchase cost and the complexity of the drive electronics, which are offset by lower operating and maintenance costs in many cases.

Stepper Motors

Stepper motors are commonly used in assembly machines for the position control of small loads at low speed (under 1,000 RPM). Positioning accuracy is determined by the number of steps in the motor, typically 200 steps, or 1.8 degrees of rotation. Microstepping drives can break these steps into 500 microsteps each, for a total resolution of 100,000 steps per revolution. However, with no motor rotor feedback, the control system cannot know when the motor stalls or misses a step, so there is no certainty that the motor has properly completed a move.

The stepper motor and drive should be sized so that the maximum torque required is no more than 50% of the rated stall torque at the operating speed. This provides room for error and unforeseen torque disturbances, so the motor should not stall. Stall detection included in the design of the control system is recommended.

Stepper motors can offer a good solution to a simple motion control problem. They are low in initial cost and are virtually maintenance free. There is a large installed base. However, with the many advances in brushless AC motor and drive technology in the last five years, there are more reasons to consider using brushless servo motor systems over stepper motors.

Servo Motor Drive Control

Most servo motion control applications are implemented with a servo motor drive control system. A servo control system consists of an actuator, feedback, and a controller acting together to control a process. In a typical servo drive control system, the actuator is a motor, the feedback is an encoder or a resolver on the motor shaft, and the controller is a signal processor and a power amplifier. The torque, speed, and position of the motor shaft are controlled. Figure 8-7 shows a block diagram of the torque and velocity loops of a typical servo motor control system. At the left in the diagram is the velocity command from the position controller and the velocity feedback from the motor shaft being summed. The result is the velocity error. This error is used by the velocity controller to generate a current command to the current controller. The

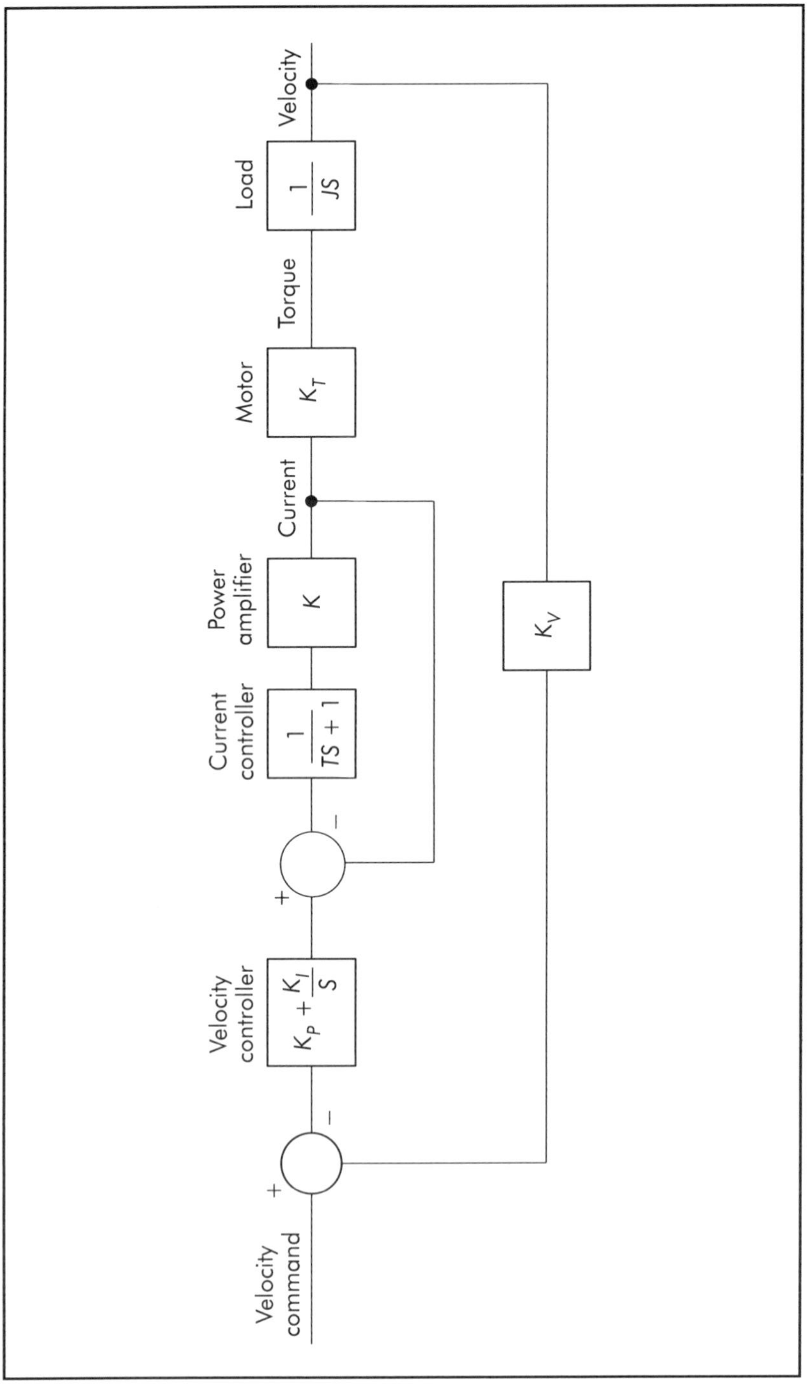

Figure 8-7. Velocity control.

current controller compares this command with the motor current feedback, and controls the motor current through the power amplifier. The motor produces a torque proportional to its current, and the motor rotor speed is proportional to the stator voltage. The current is controlled to the level needed to spin the load at the commanded velocity.

The current controller and the power amplifier are usually packaged in the same box (the motor drive) with a velocity controller. The velocity controller in the drive may or may not be used. Instead, the velocity controller may be packaged with the position controller in a computer that is optimized for high-speed, real-time control. These digital signal processing (DSP) or reduced-instruction set computing (RISC) chip-based programmable motion controllers are programmed in a high-level language. They have 20- to 100-microsecond servo loop update times, and the ability to control from one to eight motors. These motion controllers are programmed to execute motor velocity and position control loops to control the speed and position of individual motors and to coordinate the speed and position of many motors.

Figure 8-8 shows a typical position control system, which controls the motor shaft position as an outer control loop around the velocity loop. The position command is shown on the left. This is often calculated in the motion controller program, and sometimes in the program of a supervisory controller, like a PLC. It needs to be recalculated every few milliseconds while the motor is moving. The actual motor position is subtracted from the position command to create the position error. This error is used by the proportional and integral position controller to generate a velocity control signal. This control signal is added to the shaft velocity feedback, generating the velocity error. The result is the commanded velocity to the velocity controller. The output of the velocity controller is added to the motor armature current feedback. This is the command to the current amplifier that controls the motor current and voltage, and therefore the torque, velocity, and motor shaft position.

Servo drive position control systems have become very powerful in the last few years. The DSP processor has made fast processing possible, and the programming software has begun to catch up to the hardware capabilities to make these motion controllers usable. There are thousands of successful installations of these systems. They should be considered a real alternative for any stepper or DC motor application.

Coordinated Motion—Electronic Gearing

A common decision to be made in assembly machine design is how to coordinate the motion of more than one mechanism. Traditionally, mechanisms were connected through line shafts, cam shafts, rods, and

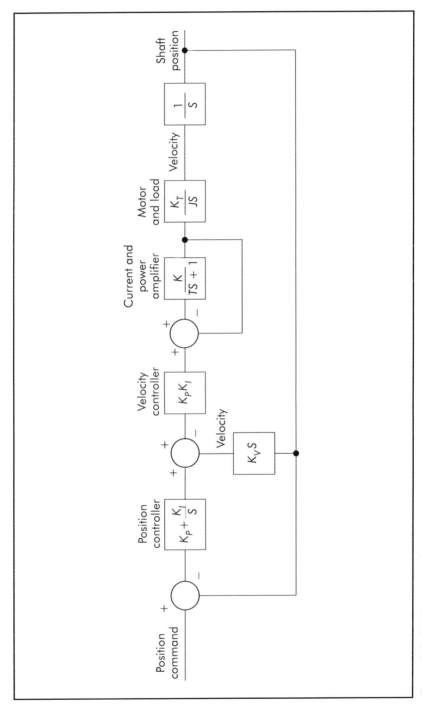

Figure 8-8. Position control system.

levers to coordinate their positions. This is no longer the only option available because of new control technology.

Servo motion control systems controlling brushless servo motors are designed to control the positions and coordinate the motions of multiple mechanisms. Most coordinated motion applications are best controlled using one of these programmable motion controllers.

A servo motion control system should be used instead of mechanical linkages when:

- The gear ratio needs to be adjustable;
- Fine tuning of positions will be needed after the machine is built;
- Axes will need to be run independently, even if only for adjustments;
- Flexibility is needed (the relationship of the axes needs to change);
- Registration control is needed (a motion controller is designed to make position corrections to moving axes at very high speeds);
- A mechanical solution is very complex.

A servo motion control system is not needed when:

- The machine movements will never change;
- Accuracy can be easily controlled mechanically;
- Plant maintenance cannot maintain a programmable motion control system, which is more complex than mechanical linkages;
- The added cost of programmable motion cannot be justified by the added features.

Summary

Motion control is a critical component of all automated machines. The decisions made about the design of the motion control system will affect all other assembly machine components, as well as the other equipment with which the machine interacts. Before the motion control system is designed, the machine requirements should be well defined as equipment specifications, and the advantages and disadvantages of the many options should be understood.

DATA ACQUISITION SYSTEM

A data acquisition system (DAS) gathers data from a process or machine, converts it to useful information and presents it to the machine operators, engineers, and production people. It is a good graphical way to get process information to a machine's operator and can help engineers manage a process. It can also build a database to facilitate production management. Data acquisition normally involves the use of a PC or minicomputer connected to a process. The computer is charged with the task of keeping track of process variables and performing trending operations. In most instances, the data is collected by the PLC that is controlling the process and sent to the DAS computer for processing. If there is no PLC used for control, the process data is brought directly into the DAS computer using digital and analog input modules.

Specifying a DAS

To design a DAS, specify the process parameters that will be logged and the ultimate use of the data. First, determine how many parameters are going to be recorded. The number of parameters will affect the size and price of the DAS. Also, define what type of signals (numeric or digital) will need to be recorded. How the data should be presented—on screen as charts or graphs, in data tables, or as a print out—should be decided. Since the data is normally stored on the PC's hard drive, define what format should be used for storage (spreadsheet, database, or raw data).

Another issue that will impact DAS performance will be whether or not it will be used for any other purposes, like real time process/machine monitoring or alarm annunciation. This may affect what kind of PC is needed and how it should be installed in the plant.

Also, it is often practical to download different process recipes from the DAS PC to the PLC. Process variable set points can be sent to the PLC to control the machine. However, a DAS PC used this way, or for any other purpose other than strictly data acquisition, may suffer from performance problems.

Minimum DAS Hardware Requirements

At a minimum, a DAS consists of a personal computer (PC) and a programmable logic controller (PLC), as shown in Figure 8-9. The PC should be equipped with a PC network connection card, CD-ROM (for most data acquisition development stations), and a large monitor.

Communications will play a large role in how well the DAS will perform. The DAS computer will have to communicate to the process PLC. On-line access to data may require more than one type of communications protocol if more than one type of PLC needs to be connected. In the end, the final destination of the data may dictate what kind of communication is required. A third piece of hardware, a printer, may be necessary if you want a hard copy of process data.

Recommendations

The following strategies are recommended for specifying DAS communications, software licensing, and system I/O.

- Use a PC network connection card, rather than a serial network, to connect the DAS PC to the machine control PLC. Serial communication has a very limited throughput, which can cause problems.

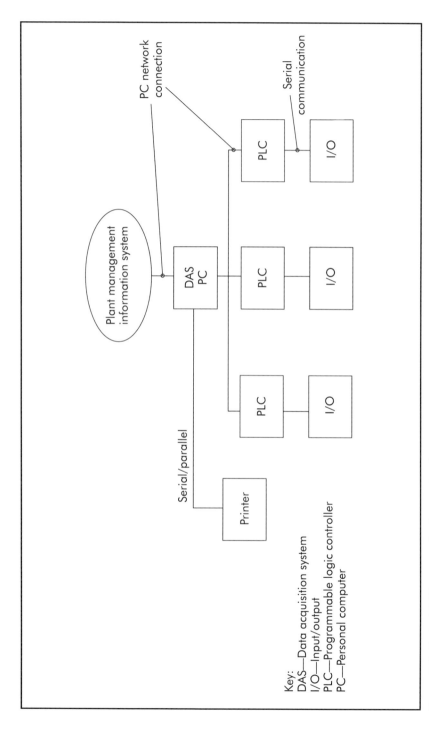

Figure 8-9. Typical DAS communications network.

- Make sure that it is consistent with the plant's other data acquisition systems and can be integrated with the plant management information system (MIS).
- Use the PLC for all system I/O. To run signals directly to a PC, it is necessary to install an additional I/O into the PC or add a data acquisition rack that feeds into a special card in the PC. Since the PLC already utilizes the process variables needed for data acquisition, separate I/O for the PC is not required.

Reports

Determine what reports are required and if they will be printed, written to disk, interfaced by spreadsheet, or sent to the plant MIS system. The format and/or style of the reports will be determined in part by who will be using them, that is, operators, supervisors, maintenance, quality assurance, or management. Each of these individuals may need different types of reports at varying frequencies.

MANUFACTURING INFORMATION SYSTEMS

Manufacturing information system (MIS) is a term that refers to the computer databases that hold the information about the processes and products in a manufacturing facility, and the systems that control that information. MIS systems are used to determine raw material needs, schedule machine production, keep track of parts in process, and gather production machine operation information. The plant MIS should include information from all of the production equipment, so assembly machines need to be connected to it.

Assembly machines are often connected to MIS systems through the actions of an operator entering machine process variables and production run data into a terminal connected to the MIS system. However, this procedure takes time the operator could use doing more productive activities. Operators make errors when entering data, and good production decisions cannot be made without accurate information. Thus, assembly machines need to be connected to the MIS system over a LAN from one of the assembly machine controllers.

Information passed from the assembly machine to the MIS system includes:

- Process variable status and history;
- Production information, such as good and reject part counts;
- Machine faults and alarm status; and
- Machine run time and downtime.

Information passed from the MIS system to the assembly machine includes:

- Product recipe and special machine configuration information;
- Number of parts to produce; and
- Production line status.

The amount and type of information sent to the MIS is determined by the needs of the plant and the capabilities of the assembly machine controllers. The needs of the plant MIS system should be determined when the control system is designed so that the assembly machine is capable of providing the information about the process that the MIS system requires.

SUMMARY

A control system provides the means to operate an assembly machine. The control system is responsible for monitoring all important machine, process, and product characteristics, coordinating its operation based upon the measured information and the control strategy designed into the machine, and reporting the status of the machine to the production personnel. The capability of control systems ranges from a machine with only manually operated actuators and no measurement, to a fully monitored and controlled machine without any operator involvement in the assembly process.

Electrical and electronic controls have become very sophisticated and much more reliable in the past few years. Computer-based controllers allow the machines to be very flexible, so that a wide variety of parts can be assembled on one machine with a change of tooling and some modifications to the controller programs. Sensors are available to measure most machine conditions, so they can be quickly shut down and repaired when there is a problem with any aspect of the operation. Parts can be fully inspected for quality during assembly and rejected when they do not meet the requirements. Computer-based CRT operator control panels provide information about the machine and the product to allow the operator, maintenance, and process engineers to keep the process running at an optimum level. Servo motion control provides a precise and much more flexible means to move and position tooling and parts than mechanical linkages. A data acquisition system connected to the plant MIS provides plant operations personnel a means to control the quality and flow of product through the entire plant.

The machine designer must decide how to best utilize these tools. The degree to which automated control is used in an assembly machine should be determined when the machine is being designed. Decisions about how to control the machine operations—manually, mechanically, or electrically—will determine the cost, complexity, and capabilities of the assembly machine. The future needs of the product and the plant should be considered when deciding upon the control strategy. The machine should be designed with the capability of having the control system upgraded as the needs of the machine change and as new control technologies are developed that will provide a better means of controlling the assembly process.

9

Machine Design Considerations

INITIAL COST COMPARED TO TOTAL COST

In addition to the functional requirements of an automated system, the designer must consider the plant environment and the ongoing costs of operating and maintaining equipment. Maintenance costs and ease of operation can have a significant impact on the total efficiency of a manufacturing system. Equipment designed to be "maintenance and operator friendly" will be better accepted, reach projected rates faster, and have lower overall operating costs. Designing such friendly features can add cost and, like most design decisions, there are tradeoffs among conflicting objectives. However, to attain higher output and reliability in new manufacturing systems, the efficiency of the plant staff is critical. Do not assume that low equipment cost is more important than ease of operation and maintenance. Be sure to consider the following when designing an automated system:

- Overload protection;
- Component life;
- Central lubrication;
- Phase adjustment;
- Antifriction bearings;
- Maintenance and operator access;
- Machine clean up;
- Quick clearing of jams; and
- Clean room or other special requirements.

ASSEMBLY BASICS

An axiom in assembly is: "never lose control of a part." For example, putting partial assemblies into a bulk container requires the addition of orientation equipment to the subsequent operation. Transferring a part from one section of a machine to another by flat-belt conveyor creates the same problem. The goal should be to minimize the number of operations, especially transfers.

Another important concept is to separate and isolate process operations. Performing a particular operation at a single station rather than using multiple tooled fixtures is good practice when designing an assembly process. Ideally, each operation is done by only one station. There are several reasons.

- An operation, such as precision insertion, can be controlled more closely if all adjustments are performed in one station. This results in a more consistent process and product.
- Better instrumentation can be justified because only one "copy" is required.
- If adjustments are required, they can be made in one location, rather than in several stations or on many fixtures.

If multiple tooled fixtures are necessary, it is worthwhile to spend time simplifying the fixtures and making them as robust as possible. Stereolithography is an excellent tool to use in the development of good fixture design. Consider how a problem with one fixture will be located and corrected during production. Is there an even number of fixtures, or will a specific fixture-to-station combination repeat only every second or third time around? Such a complex relationship is very difficult to troubleshoot.

Cam System Design Process

Three common approaches to driving automated systems are:

1. Air actuation;
2. Cam actuation; and
3. Electronic actuation.

Of these, the heavy favorite for production equipment is cam actuation. Air actuation is noisy and less reliable, and timing is difficult to maintain. Air-actuated equipment is best confined to prototypes or short-lived/lower-volume products. Electronic actuation is a very important method and is addressed in Chapter 8. It is critical that both mechanical and the latest electronic actuation technologies be understood and considered. The controls engineer must be part of the early design/decision process to ensure the best result.

Air actuation may be a good choice where actuation is needed only occasionally, say at the start of a run or at changeover. Air cylinders can be used as "air springs" to maintain a cam follower in contact, for example, when a station needs to be retracted for some operations. An air spring should be designed so that no air is consumed once it is pressurized and in normal operation. However, release of stored energy must be considered during an emergency stop. Solenoid-operated air valves are often arranged neatly in one place, such as a control panel. This creates a good appearance, but can aggravate the problem of timing air actuations due to the additional delay caused by the extra distance between the valve and the device.

Cam-actuated machines can be timed and adjusted accurately and maintain their settings better than air-actuated designs. Often, machine timing can be set at rest and will remain constant throughout the operating speed of the machine.

The cam system on a typical assembly machine has three components, as shown in Figure 9-1.

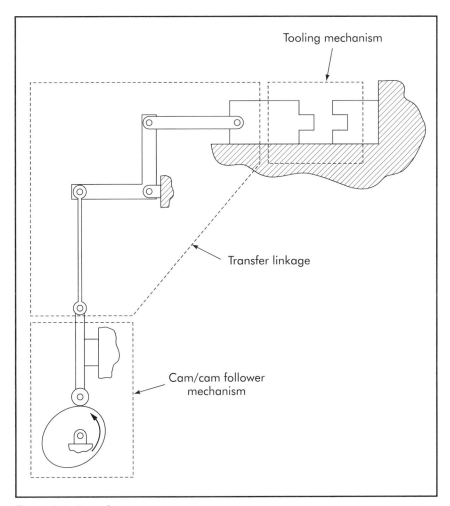

Figure 9-1. Typical cam system.

1. The tooling mechanism does the job on the assembly machine.
2. The transfer linkage enables the cam to be located away from the tooling. A series of linkages made up of connecting rods and bell-cranks transfer the cam follower motion to the tooling. This linkage must be designed to be rigid and have low backlash.
3. The cam/cam follower mechanism includes the cam, cam follower, camshaft, bearings, and drive. Some basic configurations are shown in Figure 9-2.

Table 9-1 shows mathematical functions that can be used in cam design for automated equipment. The maximum velocity, acceleration, and jerk are also given so that one motion can be compared to another.

Generally, modified sinusoidal and 3-4-5 polynomials are the best functions and should be used for all cams. However, there are exceptions to this recommendation.

- If the maximum acceleration must be kept to a minimum, then the modified trapezoidal function should be used. However, the mechanism needs to be rigid to minimize excessive vibration from the rough jerk profile.
- Cycloidal or 4-5-6-7 polynomial functions can be used if vibrations are a concern (lowest and smoothest jerk). However, the accelerations are higher.

The following sequence is generally required to design the cam system for an assembly machine.

1. Develop the timing diagram for all motions required by the tooling mechanisms on the machine.
2. Select the maximum cam diameter. In most cases, 10-12 in. (25.4-30.5 cm) allows a large enough base so that pressure angles are not a problem and allows a larger diameter camshaft. If the tooling requires motions longer than 1.5 in. (3.8 cm), selection of a larger maximum cam diameter may be required.
3. Choose the basic cam/cam follower configuration to be used on the machine. Translating roller followers and oscillating roller followers are the most common.
4. Determine camshaft location and how it is driven. The camshaft must be well supported, generally with several bearings along its length. Generally, shaft diameter should be at least 1.5 in. (3.8 cm) on shafts under 6 ft (1.8 m), and 2-3 in. (5-7.6 cm) or more on longer shafts. The final size depends on cam loads, so err toward the larger to avoid having to lay out the area later for a larger shaft (typically more difficult than going to a smaller shaft).
5. Design the kinematics of the transfer mechanisms. At this stage, the linkages are just stick figures with all pivot point locations and

Translating roller follower

In this configuration, the cam follower moves along a straight line through the axis of rotation of the cam (or perpendicular to the direction of motion for a linear cam track). This is the simplest cam system to design. However, it requires a linear slide that might not be suitable for some environments, such as a very dusty, abrasive atmosphere.

Pressure angle limit = 30°.

Translating roller follower with offset

This configuration is the same as the translating follower. However, there is one exception: the line of action of the follower motion doesn't go through the rotation axis of the cam, it is offset. This configuration is more difficult to design and, because the maximum pressure is different for the rise and the fall, it is generally used when this difference can be used as a design advantage.

Pressure angle limit = 30°.

Offset

Oscillating or pivoting roller follower

In this configuration, the cam follower is mounted on an arm that oscillates and pivots. Though slightly more difficult to design, this configuration has the advantage of allowing more aggressive cams (higher maximum pressure angles). Because there are no linear bearings, this design works well in hostile environments.

Pressure angle limit = 45°.

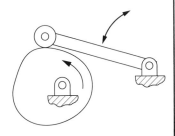

Figure 9-2. Basic cam/cam follower configurations.

Table 9-1 Math Functions for Cam Design

Function	Maximum Velocity	Maximum Acceleration	Maximum Jerk	Comments
Cycloidal	$2.000\ h/\beta$	$6.283\ h/\beta^2$	$40\ h/\beta^3$	Smooth acceleration and jerk
Trapezoidal	$2.000\ h/\beta$	$5.300\ h/\beta^2$	$44\ h/\beta^3$	Discontinuous jerk, lower speed
Modified trapezoidal	$2.000\ h/\beta$	$4.888\ h/\beta^2$	$61\ h/\beta^3$	Lowest acceleration, rough jerk
Modified sinusoidal	$1.760\ h/\beta$	$5.528\ h/\beta^2$	$69\ h/\beta^3$	Lowest velocity and pressure angle, smooth jerk, good at high speed
3-4-5 Polynomial	$1.875\ h/\beta$	$5.777\ h/\beta^2$	$60\ h/\beta^3$	Smooth jerk, good at high speed
4-5-6-7 Polynomial	$2.188\ h/\beta$	$7.526\ h/\beta^2$	$52\ h/\beta^3$	Highest acceleration, good jerk characteristics

h is total displacement (inches for translating followers and degrees for pivoting followers) of the rise or fall and β is the total time (seconds) of the rise or fall

connecting rod links determined. When laying out the transfer mechanisms, it is best to have the connecting rods and bell crank arms perpendicular to each other during the mid stroke of the mechanisms. Also, keep the rotation angle of the links and cranks small (<30°). This minimizes the distortion of cam function motion as it is transferred through the mechanisms. It also minimizes forces in the linkages and allows for the use of simple calculations when estimating mechanism forces for sizing the springs (see step 7).

6. Design each cam based on the timing diagram and the transfer linkages. Make sure that the maximum pressure angles are at or below the recommended limits, as shown in Figure 9-2. If the maximum pressure angle is too high, lower it by:

   • Using a cam motion with the lowest maximum velocity (modified sinusoidal);
   • Changing the timing diagram to allow more time for the motion;
   • Increasing cam diameter (larger base circle); or
   • Changing the cam/cam follower configuration to an oscillating style that can handle the largest maximum pressure angle.

7. Size the springs required to maintain cam/cam follower contact.

8. Determine the forces the cam is required to generate. This includes the force required to move the tooling mechanism and transfer linkage masses, the force from the return spring, and the force required by the product being assembled. Also, determine the torque required to drive the cam. Use this information to verify that the camshaft is stiff enough laterally and torsionally at each of the tooling stations to meet the desired tolerances during assembly. Unless a particular process requires more precision, it is generally recommended that maximum lateral deflection of the shaft be no more than .002-.005 in. (0.05-0.127) and torsional deflection be less than 0.10°. Redesign of the camshaft and its support may be required.

9. Perform the detailed design and engineering of each component in the cam system while keeping each component as rigid as possible. Also, ensure that the system has very little backlash.

The following features should be incorporated into all cam systems.

• Split cams are a must for most machines because maintenance should never have to remove the camshaft to replace a cam.
• Use springs to maintain cam/cam follower contact at all but the slowest machine speeds. This is true even if tracked or grooved cams are used. Tracked cams without a spring cause the cam follower to jump from one side of the track to the other. This causes shock, vibration, and excessive cam and follower wear. Use tracked

cams only to prevent machine crashes in the case of spring failure. The only exception to this recommendation is conjugate cams. *Conjugate cams* are pairs of cam surfaces and cam followers designed so that at least one of the cams is always pushing, making cam float impossible. Conjugate cams are rare because of the additional design effort required, but are used in very high-speed equipment, such as printing presses.

- On higher speed machines where a rise motion is followed immediately with a return (no dwell), maintain acceleration through the rise-return transition. This avoids unnecessary return to zero acceleration. This technique improves the smoothness of the jerk throughout the cycle, and allows for slightly more aggressive cam motion. The design requires a general polynomial or double harmonic cam motion function. The maximum accelerations of these motions can be higher than if the standard cam functions are used.
- Circular interpolation is required for smooth cam surfaces during computer-numerical control (CNC) machining. Not all shops are aware of this.
- On very highly loaded cams, use a yoke-mounted cam follower that can pivot slightly to align to the cam surface. This minimizes contact stress in the cam and increases the life of the cam and cam follower.

Overload Protection

Good overload protection is probably the most effective way to minimize downtime caused by jams and crashes. Design individual stations to allow for jams, double parts, and other overloads without damaging the machine. Stations that are easy to clear and fast to reset minimize lost production.

The two basic types of overload devices are self-resetting and nonself-resetting. It is important that the operator know immediately when an overload device trips, and be able to identify the tripped device quickly. Overload devices must be equipped with a detection system to indicate their status.

Locate clutches and other overload devices as close to the jam point as possible. This localizes the effect of the jam on the equipment and optimizes the sensitivity of the overload device. The operator should be able to reset overload devices quickly, without tools.

Component Life

Components in an automated machine should be capable of operating for at least 10 years without replacement. Those that are subject to wear or failure should be designed for quick change and included in the spare parts provided with the machine. When selecting components, set the operating range between 50% and 75% of the component rating to provide a greater safety margin and longer life.

Central Lubrication

Most automated equipment is designed with permanently lubricated bearings. If lubrication is required, a central lubrication system is desirable. Since over-lubrication can be just as detrimental as under-lubrication, use a metering device to regulate the flow of lubrication to each point. Be sure to consider the possibility of product contamination in the design of any mechanism located above the product work plane. Design equipment so that lubrication can be accomplished without interrupting operation.

Maintenance and Operator Access

As mentioned earlier, maximum productivity is dependent upon quick restart after a jam or failure. Providing adequate access allows problems to be corrected as quickly as possible. Recommended access and horizontal work clearances are shown in Figures 9-3 and 9-4.

Related considerations include:

- Incorporate ample chamfer (preferred for low cost) or radii on corners and edges;
- Minimize the number of screws required to attach components, especially guards;
- Use hinged guarding wherever possible;
- Use tool-free or quarter-turn fasteners on guards that are removed frequently or periodically and be sure the guards have electrical interlocks;
- Use machined shapes (preferred) or pilot pins that provide self-alignment for accuracy and ease of reinstallation for fixturing and station tooling;
- Use fasteners that can be removed with standard tools;
- Design equipment so that product height is in the comfortable working zone for operators; and
- Provide adequate space between adjacent stations for operator and maintenance access.

Machine Cleanup

As causes of downtime are eliminated, machine cleanup remains a source of downtime on most equipment. For safety reasons, a machine must be shut down during cleanup. Therefore, the only way to reduce this cause of downtime is to design the equipment for quick, easy cleaning.

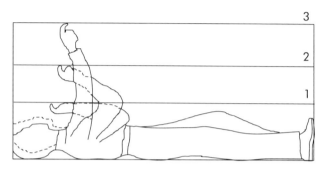

| | Minimum Dimensions | |
Position	Vertical in. (cm)	Horizontal in. (cm)
1. Lying for inspection.	18 (46)	76 (193)
2. Restricted space for small tools and minor adjustments: power front elbow extension not possible.	24 (61)	76 (193)
3. Space for reasonable arm extension: power tools with a length of 6-8 in. (15-20 cm) could be used.	32 (81)	76 (193)

The minimum horizontal space of 76 in. (193 cm) for a person in the supine position (on the back) will accommodate most people comfortably.

The vertical clearance dimensions (1, 2, and 3) vary with the tasks to be performed. More space is needed (2 and 3) if the arms have to exert force for use of tools.

Dimension data developed from information contained in Croney 1971; Hertzberg, Emanuel, and Alexander 1956; Rigby, Cooper, and Spickard,1961; and Kodak 1983.

Figure 9-3. Minimum horizontal work area clearances.

Minimal two-hand access openings without visual access

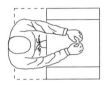

Reaching with both hands to a depth of 6 to 19.25 in. (15-49 cm)

Light clothing:	width	8 in. (20 cm) or the depth of reach
	height	5 in. (13 cm)
Arctic clothing:	width	6 in. (15 cm) plus ¾ the depth of reach
	height	7 in. (18 cm)

Reaching full arm's length (to shoulders) with both arms

width	19.5 in. (50 cm)
height	5 in. (13 cm)

Inserting box grasped by handles on the front

2 in. (5 cm) clearance around the box, assuming adequate clearance around handles

Inserting box with hands on the sides

Light clothing:	width	box plus 4.5 in. (11 cm)
	height*	5 in. (13 cm) high or .5 in. (1.3 cm) around box (whichever is larger)
Arctic clothing:	width	box plus 7 in. (18 cm)
	height*	8.5 in. (22 cm) high or .5 in. (1.3 cm) around box (whichever is larger)

*If hands curl around bottom, allow an extra 1.5 in. (4 cm) for light clothing and 3 in. (8 cm) for arctic clothing

Figure 9-4. Hand and arm access dimensions.

Minimal one-hand access openings without visual access

Empty hand to wrist

Bare hand, rolled: 3.75 in. (9.5 cm) square or diameter

Bare hand, flat: 2.25 in. height × 4 in. width (6 cm × 10 cm) or 4 in. (10 cm) in diameter

Glove or mitten: 4 in. height × 6 in. width (10 cm × 15 cm) or 6 in. (15 cm) in diameter

Arctic mitten: 5 in. height × 6.5 in. width (13 cm × 17 cm) or 6.5 in. (17 cm) in diameter

Clenched hand to wrist

Bare hand: 3.5 in. height × 5 in. width (9 cm × 13 cm) or 5 in. (13 cm) in diameter

Glove or mitten: 4.5 in. height × 6 in. width (11 cm × 15 cm) or 6 in. (15 cm) in diameter

Arctic mitten: 7 in. height × 8.5 in. width (18 cm × 22 cm) or 8.5 in. (22 cm) in diameter

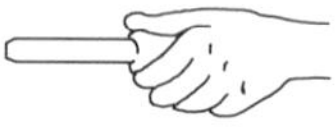

Hand plus 1 in. (2.5 cm) diameter object to wrist

Bare hand: 3.75 in. (9.5 cm) square or diameter

Gloved hand: 6 in. (15 cm) square or diameter

Arctic mitten: 7 in. (18 cm) square or diameter

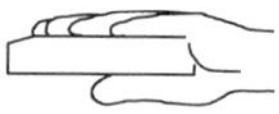

Hand plus object over 1 in. (2.5 cm) diameter to wrist

Bare hand: 1.75 in. (4.4 cm) clearance around object

Glove or mitten: 2.5 in. (6 cm) clearance around object

Arctic mitten: 3.5 in. (9 cm) clearance around object

Arm to elbow

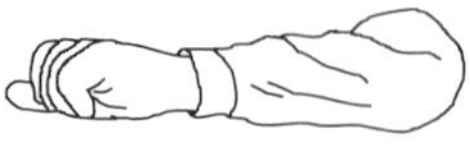

Light clothing: 4 in. height × 4.5 in. width (10 cm × 11 cm) or 4.5 in. (11 cm) in diameter

Arctic clothing: 7 in. (18 cm) square or diameter

With object: clearance as above

Figure 9-4. Continued.

Minimal one-hand access openings without visual access *(continued)*

Arm to shoulder
    Light clothing: 5 in. (13 cm) square or diameter
    Arctic clothing: 8.5 in. (22 cm) square or diameter
    With object: clearance as above

Minimal finger access to first joint

Push-button access
    Bare hand: 1.25 in. (3.2 cm) diameter
    Gloved hand: 1.5 in. (4 cm) diameter
Two-finger twist access
    Bare hand: object plus 2 in. (5 cm) in diameter
    Gloved hand: object plus 2.5 in. (6 cm) in diameter

Figure 9-4. Continued.

Some design considerations are:

- Avoid horizontal surfaces below the product path;
- Allow a clear space below the product path so debris falls to the floor and not into the machine;
- Allow broom clearance under the machine;
- Design machine legs for easy cleaning;
- Enclose the machine framework to allow cleanup with a pressurized air nozzle (except in clean room environments); and
- Provide a "home" position for any dispensing nozzles that could drip when idle.

Quick Clearing of Jams

Jams are a major cause of downtime on most automated machines, and operators are slower to respond to those that take longer to clear. Reducing the average time to restart a machine after a jam is an effective way of improving run time. This can be best addressed during initial design. Feed tracks, nests, and fixtures can be designed with quick-opening features, as shown in Figure 9-5.

Figure 9-6 shows how a toggle clamp in the closed position provides a rigid mount for the tooling. The toggle is easy to open and provides clear access in the open position. Opening the cover plate automatically disengages the detent, as shown in Figure 9-7.

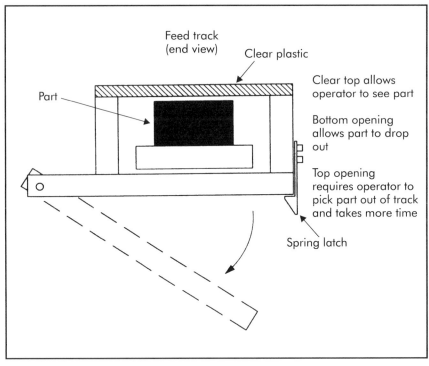

Figure 9-5. Quick-clearing design features.

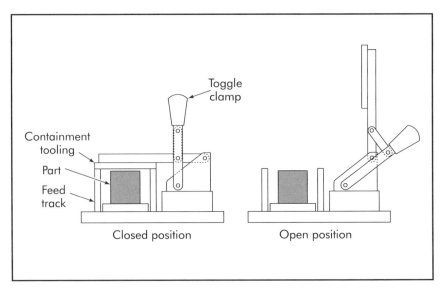

Figure 9-6. Toggle clamp.

Where maximum rigidity is not required, a spring loaded detent can be used as shown in Figure 9-7 or a spring or magnetic latch on the door may suffice, as shown in Figures 9-8 and 9-9.

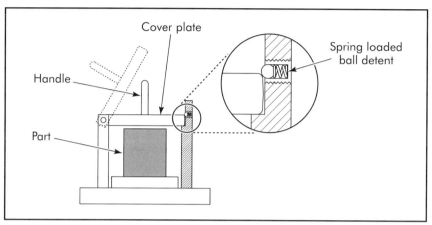

Figure 9-7. Detent.

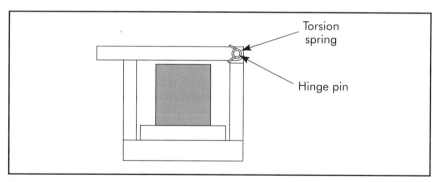

Figure 9-8. Spring.

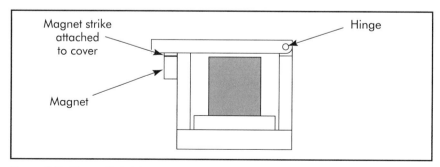

Figure 9-9. Magnetic latch.

Additional considerations:

- Provide a complete backup system either off-line or on-line in an adjacent station; and
- Provide handles or manual advance wheels so the operator can move the drive forward or back to clear the jam.

POWER TRANSMISSION

Maintaining exact timing relationships throughout an assembly machine at all speeds is critical. Using cams and shafts allows timing to be set at rest and remain constant at any speed.

A gearbox or silent chain best accomplishes transfer of power from one shaft to another. Timing belts are a good choice in many applications where slightly less stiffness can be tolerated.

Roller chains are generally a poor choice and should not be used on high-speed or precision applications. They introduce vibration due to the cordal action of the links, especially when using small sprockets and/or larger chain sizes. Roller chains also tend to be dirty and require frequent adjustment due to wear.

Pneumatic-powered actuation should be avoided on high-speed or precision assembly. Timing the actuation of pneumatic systems is difficult and speed-dependent. Compressed air is expensive and usually creates additional noise. If pneumatic devices are used, provide filters and separators at the machine and mufflers on exhausts. Consider hydraulics where a flexible power source is needed, such as for a pressing or forming operation.

Drive Train Stiffness

Accurate timing of various operations in an assembly machine requires minimum deflection in the connections between stations. In other words, an assembly machine drive train must be stiff.

Dynamic loading in a complex assembly operation can cause flexion in the drive system that alters assembly function timing. This happens all too frequently and is an indication that designers need to pay more attention to drive train stiffness. For a given drive layout, a larger drive shaft diameter is one way to reduce torsional deflection; higher modulus of elasticity material is another.

Figure 9-10 shows examples of two loads connected by different drive-train designs. Design (a) is a low-speed, 200-RPM drive train; design (b) is a high-speed, 1,000-RPM drive train with reducers at each workstation. Assuming the shafts are the same size, the drive train with reducers (b) is preferred because it is "stiffer" than design (a) and, therefore, maintains more accurate timing between the two loads.

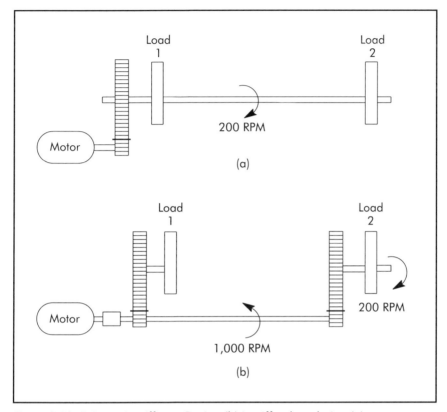

Figure 9-10. Drive train stiffness. Design (b) is stiffer than design (a).

MACHINE ADJUSTMENTS

Slotted adjustment methods should generally be avoided in favor of more positive methods. Figures 9-11, 9-12, 9-13, and 9-14 show some simple yet positive adjustment methods. Where adjustments occur frequently, a handwheel can be provided to minimize the need for tools. If the adjustment requires accuracy or if a number of operation set points are required, provide either a digital readout indicator or a pointer and scale. Where frequent or rapid changeovers are necessary, adjustments can be servo driven.

Figure 9-11 shows the tooling is located with a combination of a jackscrew and a captured compression spring in a spring-loaded configuration. This is the preferred method of adjustment unless absolute rigidity is required. The compression spring provides compliancy during adjustment and must be sized for the particular application. The compression spring can provide overload protection if needed.

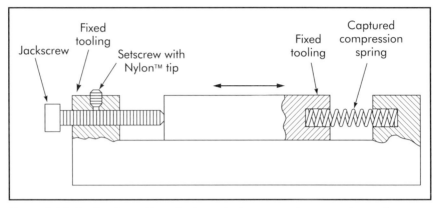

Figure 9-11. Tooling is positioned using a jackscrew and compression spring.

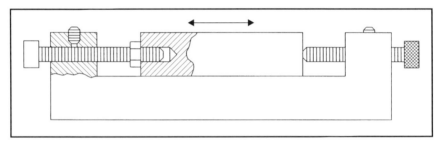

Figure 9-12. Tooling is positioned using a pair of jackscrews.

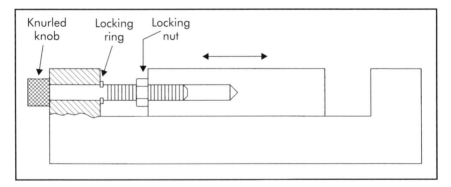

Figure 9-13. Tooling is positioned using a simple jackscrew.

Figure 9-12 shows the tooling located with a pair of jackscrews in a push-push configuration. This method provides maximum rigidity, but requires more time to perform an adjustment. The push-push configuration should be selected over the spring-loaded configuration when absolute rigidity is required and compliancy is not required.

The preceding figures show a setscrew with a nylon tip for locking. Other means of locking the jackscrew include a locking nut or compression spring between the jackscrew head and the fixed tooling. Figure 9-13 shows tooling in a push-pull configuration. This push-pull configuration works well with tooling under light loading conditions. If a digital readout indicator is required, the jackscrew can be replaced with a threaded rod, as shown in Figure 9-14.

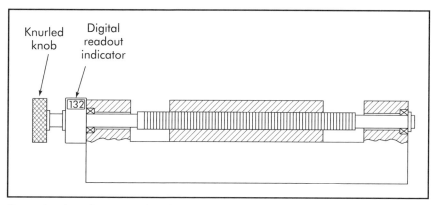

Figure 9-14. Jackscrew replaced with a threaded rod.

ARE COSMETICS IMPORTANT?

Customer (plant) acceptance of new equipment begins long before the equipment is installed and operational. It begins when the designer first accepts and incorporates input from the plant and when the plant is first exposed to the new equipment.

Cosmetics help shape first impressions and, for this reason, they are very important. The "customer" is anyone who will be involved with the equipment on an ongoing basis. Cosmetics influence the customer's initial attitude toward the equipment, and cosmetics help determine whether the customer will be enthusiastic or skeptical during startup. Customer involvement also increases the enthusiasm with which the equipment is received.

A machine that looks good—clean design, good workmanship, operator-friendly layout—is the product of a designer who pays attention to detail. It is the result of a design that combines functionality and cosmetics. This is not to say that every new idea should be incorporated causing project costs to soar out of control. *Creeping elegance* is a descriptive term for a project that grows beyond what is required or justified.

It is important to consider all design elements as early as possible, including those that are implemented near the end of machine assembly.

Guards

Guards are not an add-on feature. They must blend in with other design elements, including the frame, and they must be planned early in the process. Planning involves adopting a general guarding philosophy, such as employing bolt-on guards, interlocked doors, and light curtains. Guarding details are often determined later, near the end of assembly, or after specific operator access requirements have been determined. This often occurs during shop debug. Guards can sometimes be avoided by designing machine elements to be intrinsically safe.

Noise Control

Not all cosmetic influences are visible. For instance, the noise level of a machine could be considered a cosmetic feature as well as a safety consideration. A quiet machine is a reflection of good design. In fact, excessive noise could be an indication of hard stops, followers lifting off cams, or other design problems. Continuous motion machines are significantly quieter than intermittent motion machines—especially intermittent motion assembly machines that use air cylinders for the placement process.

DESIGN SIMPLICITY

Good designs are simple, and simplification becomes more important as speed increases. However, achieving simplicity is not easy. It is far more difficult to produce a simple design that works than it is to produce a complex design that accomplishes the same task. It has been said that "any fool can make something complicated—it takes talent to make something very simple."

EFFECT OF MECHANICAL DESIGN ON CONTROLLABILITY

Although the machine control system is often the responsibility of a controls engineer, mechanical systems must be designed with control in mind. Not only should the controls engineer be involved early in the equipment development process (concurrent engineering), but the mechanical designer also should have a good understanding of sound controls practice.

One important concept is that of collocated versus noncollocated control. As an example, let's assume a rotary dial is to be positioned accurately. A servo motor controls the dial with a belt connecting the motor to it. Where should the sensor (probably an encoder) be placed? If it is placed on the dial, the result is a noncollocated system. The sensor and motor are separated by a dynamic or "flexible" element (the belt). As gain is increased, the system becomes unstable. Noncollocated control should be avoided if possible. If the sensor is located on the motor, the result is a collocated system. The control system is inherently stable, but dial position accuracy may be compromised due to flexibility in the belt. The best choice in this example is probably to locate the encoder on the servo motor and use a sufficiently stiff transmission element to guarantee the required accuracy at the dial. This example shows the importance of considering controls and controllability during mechanical design and not as a separate, sequential task. More information on controls is in Chapter 8.

SUMMARY

To keep equipment costs low, features that can make the actual operation easier are often not considered. However, if the objective is to optimize long-term return-on-investment, it may be wise to spend a little more to make the operators and maintenance as efficient as possible. Features such as ergonomic design, quick clean-out, and easy access, provide a pay back on a daily basis for the life of the equipment. These features, combined with a good, clean appearance, have a significant effect on maintenance and the attitude of operators. Attitude can make a big difference in how well a new system is accepted and how quickly the equipment becomes productive.

10

Debug, Checkout, and Startup

DEFINITIONS

Debug: To search for and eliminate malfunctioning elements.
Checkout: A test of a machine for proper functioning.
Startup: The act of initiating a process.

THE DEBUG, CHECKOUT, AND STARTUP PROCESSES

The debug, checkout, and startup processes are often much more complex than expected, especially when assembly equipment is involved. These processes are highly stressful but also rewarding periods of a project. Many conflicting objectives must be dealt with. For example, a very thorough debug at the assembly shop may take longer, but reduces problems during plant startup. Usually during this time, there is pressure to ship equipment to the plant so that it can start operating and producing revenue sooner. The right trade-off between cost and time during these processes can maximize progress toward business objectives. It is very difficult to know the correct balance, although there is usually no shortage of opinions. One major reason these decisions are so difficult is that cost is immediate and certain, while benefit is future and uncertain.

Some questions that should be answered early are the following:

- When and to what extent should maintenance become involved?
- When and to what extent should operators become involved?
- How many of each component will be consumed?
- What will the costs be for components consumed during debug and checkout?
- Will any of the components or products be saleable?
- If some product is saleable, what are the release standards and who will be responsible?

Some of the most successful checkouts and startups have resulted from allowing production operators to actually run the equipment during these phases on the assembly shop floor.

Debug is very much like invention—it is hard to predict how long it will take. If the assembly process is new and difficult, it will take longer. If prototyping was used effectively earlier to tune the process, it will take less time. Each machine creates a new experience.

Figure 10-1 illustrates debug, checkout, and startup process complexity. The process starts with mechanical and electrical engineers working together on the assembly shop floor. It ends with operators running the equipment and producing saleable product. Obviously, a major transition in responsibility and roles must occur.

Under the best conditions, the shop acceptance run meets all performance requirements and the machine is shipped on schedule. If this is not the case, business requirements must determine what performance level is acceptable. If the business requires 100% and this level has not yet been reached, the machine should not be shipped. However, if product is needed to satisfy customers it may be wiser to ship, even if the machine meets less than 100% of the performance requirements. Many decisions at this project stage are judgement calls. Decisions regarding safety may be the only decisions not subject to compromise.

In general, shipping a machine before it meets the shop acceptance criteria should be avoided. Correcting problems is generally much easier in the shop where the equipment and human resources are available. The difficulty of completing checkout in the plant is often underestimated because plant staff usually has production responsibilities and working on new equipment is a second priority.

Figure 10-1 shows that machine performance does not necessarily improve constantly and steadily throughout the processes. During shop debug, problems stop progress until they are solved. However, machine output often increases sharply after a key breakthrough. This is the nature of debug. Usually, a reduction in performance is perceived when the equipment is started up in the plant. Although there certainly can be actual drops in performance, the drop often results from changing the time period being measured. Shop acceptance is typically a series of 1 or 2-hour runs, whereas plant acceptance time is usually longer. As the measurement period gets longer, it becomes more difficult to maintain the same performance level.

A dip in performance is often seen at A2 (plant checkout), as shown in Figure 10-1. This dip is the learning curve of relatively new operators being "on their own." There is a learning curve each time the responsibility for operating the equipment is transferred to a new individual or crew. The more that maintenance and operators are involved during the debug and checkout, the less the impact on machine performance when the transfer of responsibility occurs.

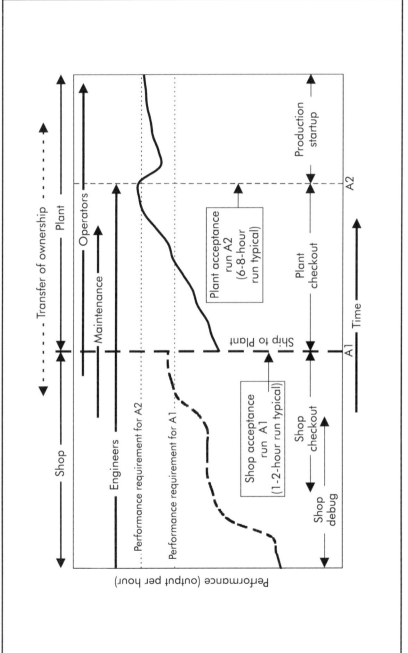

Figure 10-1. Machine performance during debug, checkout, and startup.

THE IMPORTANCE OF A CROSS-FUNCTIONAL TEAM

If there is any one time in the life of a challenging automated assembly project where a cross-functional team is the most beneficial, it is during the debug, checkout, and startup processes. Decisions relating to the trade-off between technical and business goals must be made, and only a well functioning team can make the best choices. Without a good team, it is easy to fall into finger-pointing or create adversarial relationships when good cooperation is most critical. A project team that has worked together through an entire project will be able to make the right choices to optimize both short- and long-term business objectives.

THE DEBUGGING STEP

In a study of 18 manufacturing plants, the debugging step was found to be the major source of difficulty in the equipment acquisition process (Riley 1983). The debugging process on automated assembly equipment usually requires much more effort than that required on other equipment. It is important to allow for this when planning an automation project.

Whether equipment is built in-house or by a supplier, delays and problems during the debug step can be minimized by anticipating and handling these difficulties early in the project. Good working relationships between special equipment procurement staffs, product design departments, and suppliers of equipment are necessary for long-term success. It is advantageous to restrict the number of suppliers selected and to develop close cooperation with them (Riley 1983). The next few sections discuss techniques and ideas that help minimize the debugging step.

Equipment and Process Failure

The debugging step is characterized by two basic problems:

1. Equipment failure; and
2. Process failure.

Figure 10-2 shows a normal "bathtub" failure curve for devices such as bearings and switches.

Although irritating and occasionally difficult to locate, equipment failures are generally far less troublesome than process failures. Since equipment failures are usually caused by faulty components or premature component failure, the solution is early "run in" or "burn in." That is, operate the equipment as long as practical within the limits of safety (24-hour minimum recommended) without any products or processing material. During this period, premature equipment failures can be corrected in the shop.

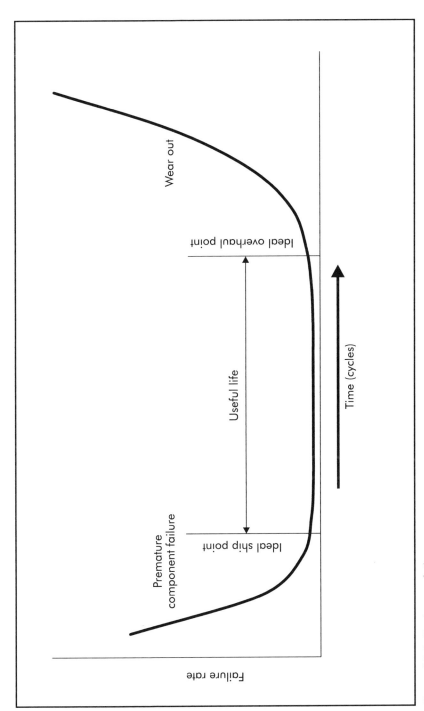

Figure 10-2. Equipment failure curve.

Process failures usually consume 90%+ of the debugging effort. These include inconsistent transfers and placements, jams, quality rejects, and similar occurrences. The way to minimize process failures is to pay close attention to the details during equipment planning and design.

Although some debugging is probably inevitable, the target should be *zero debug* at final assembly. One useful technique is to test and debug as thoroughly as possible, each subsection of the machine as it is completed. This is especially worthwhile on complex systems. Time is saved even if a slightly different approach may be needed to design and plan each subsection so that it can be driven and controlled separately during debugging.

Determine the quantities of parts needed for debugging early in the project. Provide a cost estimate and schedule delivery of needed parts with the plant or parts suppliers. Use production-quality parts that are within specification for debugging; never use scrap parts for debug. Debugging while using scrap parts is seldom valid and usually wastes valuable time.

At this point, compare current parts with parts received during the early design phase. Previously acquired component data, such as that described in Chapter 2 *"Part Variability,"* will prove valuable in identifying what has changed. Considerable time can be saved by comparing old and new parts, since much of the debugging effort is spent adjusting for part changes.

OPTIMIZATION AND TROUBLESHOOTING

Use these techniques and procedures to ensure that debug and checkout are orderly and successful.

Maintain Level of Machine

Perform the following when readying equipment for shipment from the builder's floor after it has been qualified, but *before it is moved.*

1. Measure the pitch of the machine table using a precision level (.0005 in./ft [0.416 mm/m]).
2. Record the measurement.
3. Scribe a line around the level so a measurement can be taken from the same location when the machine is in place on the plant floor.
4. Repeat steps one through three at various locations on the machine table.
5. Level the machine on the plant floor reproducing the measurements taken at the locations recorded in the earlier steps (1-4).

Use High-speed Video

Record the checkout of all assembly operations using a high-speed video camera. Viewing the placement and assembly operation in slow motion makes it much easier to detect trouble spots or marginal operations. It also makes the effect of changes more obvious.

Inspect and Record Reject Parts

During checkout, inspect all rejected parts that come off an assembly machine. Record cavity or tool numbers. Rejects are often from one or two cavities, indicating that something is different about parts from these cavities.

Number Machine Nests

Number each *nest* (the tooling that holds the product) on a multiple-nest machine, including spare nests. When a problem occurs, perform a nest study on the machine to detect the problem nest(s).

Check for Residual Magnetism

When troubleshooting a machine that assembles steel parts, look for signs of residual magnetism in any tooling finished by a surface grinder. It is good practice to demagnetize all surface-ground parts.

Make Changes During Checkout Systematically

Avoid making wholesale changes during checkout. Modifications should be made one at a time and the results analyzed before moving on. Concentrate on one machine operation at a time, starting with the most basic or first operation in a sequence. Debugging a complex system can, at first, seem overwhelming. A step-by-step, methodical approach may appear slow, but is almost always faster in the end.

Debug One Station at a Time

If the equipment is driven by one power source, such as a line shaft, disconnect the power takeoff to all undebugged stations or remove station tooling to concentrate on one station at a time.

Debug Mechanical and Electrical Systems Together

Complete the programmable logic controller (PLC) debug in conjunction with the mechanical debug. The controls engineer or programmer should be available during all debug phases.

ACCEPTANCE RUN

The acceptance run is a critical step in any automated assembly project. It is usually a series of runs for different product or process conditions. Although it is important to establish acceptance criteria early in the project, it is very common to make some modifications at the time of acceptance. The cost and availability of quality parts are factors that often affect the length of acceptance runs. Regardless of the changes necessary, keep accurate records of all acceptance runs. Figure 10-3 shows a form used for documenting acceptance runs.

It is good practice to limit the people allowed in the area during the acceptance run. For purchased equipment, the supplier's engineer and the purchasing engineer should be the only people allowed in the area—with the possible exception of someone to record the results. Each failure should be evaluated and the cause recorded. Adjustments to machine settings should not be made during an acceptance run. If adjustments are necessary, the acceptance run should be restarted. A methodical approach to acceptance results in a better picture of true machine condition relative to expectations. An acceptance run is a managed formal event and should be planned and staffed accordingly.

DOCUMENTATION, TRAINING, AND FOLLOWUP

The ease and time required for a new system to reach its potential is very dependent on effective hand off between engineers and plant staff. Good documentation is the foundation of the plant's learning curve. The elements of a good equipment manual are shown in Table 10-1.

Information transfer should begin in earnest during the checkout phase. Engineers should give a training session when the equipment is in the plant, but prior to startup. The entire system should be covered in detail, including the reasoning behind design choices, as well as the theory behind any new processes. However, initial training is not enough. A follow-up training session 2 months after startup should be part of the project plan. Experience has shown that after about 2 months the plant staff will not only have a number of questions, but usually will be very receptive to a thorough review. There is generally too much new information to absorb everything in the first training session. After working with the system for a while, the plant staff will be able to absorb more of the information. Thorough training of plant staff has two major benefits:

1. It minimizes the time engineers have to spend on followup activities; and
2. It upgrades plant staff skills on current equipment and develops a higher skill level in support of future projects.

ACCEPTANCE TEST LOG

File No:

Machine name:

Operators: Date of test:

Recorder: Time of test:

Acceptance criteria: Page   of

Machine settings: (list all adjustable features and current setting)

Input materials: (list all input materials and all available information including date of manufacture, lot number, etc.)

Figure 10-3. Acceptance test log.

Summary of test

Machine speed:	Total output:
Total time of test:	Rejects:
Less nonchargeable downtime:	Good output:
Net time of test:	% Yield:
Chargeable downtime:	
Run time:	
% Run time:	
Results/comments:	

Time	Event	Chargeable downtime	Nonchargeable downtime	Comments

Figure 10-3. Continued.

Table 10-1. Recommended Outline for a New Equipment Manual

Section	Contents
Machine characteristics	Machine description, materials processed, product produced, component identification diagram, controls and indicators, operator control panel, and description of operating modes.
Installation	Pre-installation check list, unpacking, setup, checkout, and machine configuration work sheet (all values recorded at installation).
Adjustments	Procedures organized by machine area, then by subassembly.
Maintenance	Required tools, test equipment and supplies, preventive and emergency maintenance procedures, removal and replacement procedures organized by machine area, then by subassembly.
Theory of operation	Overview from machine-on to machine-off, descriptions and flow diagrams organized by machine area, then by subassembly.
Troubleshooting	Typical problems, causes, suggested remedial action, and diagnostics.
Electrical diagrams	Wiring diagrams and schematics.
Parts	Parts list, recommended spares, sources, and exploded views keyed to parts list.

SUMMARY

The debug, checkout, and startup processes of an automated assembly system are complex, demanding, dynamic, stressful, and rewarding. It is a time of ownership transition from engineers to plant operators and maintenance personnel. Good planning and teamwork during the project pay off during startup. If problems do arise, the team is in the best position to resolve them.

REFERENCES

Riley, Frank J. 1983. *Assembly Automation: A Management Handbook*. New York: Industrial Press: 17.

Appendix A
Miscellaneous Tips

The following collection of tips is offered from experienced automation engineers.

AUTOMATED ASSEMBLY

- Simplify the product and refine the process first, then automate.
- The first venture from manual assembly into automated assembly is the most difficult.
- Automated assembly should be addressed as a system, and all parts of that system should be optimized to achieve the maximum system efficiency.
- Achieving an optimum manufacturing system usually requires product and process modifications
- Manual assembly is forgiving of component variability and defects; automatic assembly is not forgiving.
- Automating an assembly operation improves quality, but requires higher quality components.
- Assume parts don't match blueprint designs and specifications 100%—they almost never do.
- Always critically evaluate components for assembly by measuring them.
- If any defective components are found, beware of the defect level.
- Even a relatively low level of defects causes high downtime.
- Plant personnel often don't know the defect level of components. Determine or estimate the defect level early in the project so that any problems can be addressed.
- If the defect level is measured as a percentage, the defect level is probably too high for successful automation.
- The most effective way to increase uptime is to reduce the time to restart.
- Target 40 defects per million parts or less for operations running up to 100 parts per minute (less for higher speeds).
- No matter how good an assembly operation is, it can be made better by improving the consistency of input materials.
- Experiment and prototype (quick and simple) early on. "Do a little —learn a little."
- Automating requires development—don't underestimate time.
- Plan for inspection from the start, and install or leave space.

- Determine the design and build supplier early (before the prototype stage, if possible).
- Take the time for design reviews, call in experts, get into detail.
- If your intuition makes you uncomfortable—watch out, check it out. Your experience is trying to tell you something.
- Each transfer, such as a walking beam, has a reliability factor.
- Machine and drive stiffness is essential to maintain timing accuracy.
- Anticipate the quantity and cost of product needed for checkout.

COMPONENT FEEDING

- The track for a vibratory in-line feeder should be one piece, if possible, and either level or sloped down in the direction of part travel. If one-piece construction is not possible, allow a slight downstream drop between track sections (.003-.005 in. [0.076-0.127 mm]), with less for very small parts. A slight flare or chamfer on the sides is also recommended. Alignment pins or gage blocks should be supplied with the feeder system.
- Assume that bulk parts contain debris. Design the bowl and feedtrack so debris falls through and does not reach the next operation.
- Provide sufficient feed track to act as a buffer in the event of a jam in the feeder.
- One of the rules of good automation is to orient and handle each part only once if possible.

GENERAL DESIGN

Tips for general design include considerations for:

- Stress-relieve parts;
- Bolt instead of weld;
- Special air cylinders;
- Part weight;
- Compression versus extension springs;
- Designing in sensors;
- Ball bearing designs;
- Marking parts;
- Couplings;
- Linkage bearings;
- Rapid prototyping;
- Leveling pads; and
- Color-coding the change parts.

Stress-relieve Parts

Always stress-relieve welded components, such as machine frames. When installing a tabletop on a frame, install pads on top of the frame for bolting on the tabletop. After stress-relieving the parts, machine all pads in the same plane for a flat, accurate tabletop.

Bolt Instead of Weld

Use bolted construction versus welded construction. Weldments are prone to "move" during machining due to internal stresses. Bolted construction allows for alignment and changes as needed during assembly. If weldments are used, make them very simple.

Special Air Cylinders

If an air cylinder is required to cycle frequently or if low breakaway force is desired, consider using a dashpot. Since dashpots do not have seals, some air leakage will occur. However, they may provide a solution in lower force applications.

Noting Part Weight

During equipment design, it is beneficial to note the weight of the machine parts that move on the drawing. This allows for quickly determining the weight of an assembly for sizing cams, air cylinders, and so on.

Compression versus Extension Springs

Use compression springs instead of extension springs wherever possible. The hook of the extension spring is a high-stress area and is more susceptible to failure.

Designing in Sensors

Incorporate sensor locations in the machine design as early as possible. Waiting until the end delays the startup and it can be difficult to find locations to mount sensors properly.

Ball Bearing Race Designs

Use ball bearings with extended internal races and shoulder or snap-ring external races as shown in Figure A-1. These have the following advantages:

- Eliminate machined shoulders;
- Eliminate spacers;
- Eliminate machining two bores when using two bearings on a common shaft;
- Fewer parts; and
- Easier to assemble and disassemble.

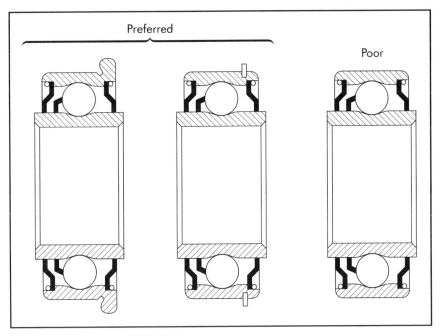

Figure A-1. Ball bearing race designs.

Marking Parts

Mark assemblies or wear parts with part numbers (stamped into metal). This saves time in finding replacement parts or documentation. Also, some parts may require marks for orientation to ensure that they are installed correctly. Make these marks in the part during fabrication.

Couplings

Use torsionally rigid couplings on servo and stepper motors. The bellows type is best.

Linkage Bearings

Use needle bearings and rolling-element trust bearings in the joints of linkages. They have the highest load rating for their size. Also, use oversized shafts (for example, oversized dowel pins) when using needle bearings to reduce slop in the linkage.

Rapid Prototyping

Use a rapid prototyping system, such as stereolithography, to build early prototype parts and forms for investment casting of production tooling.

Leveling Pads

Use commercial machine leveling pads instead of bolts. They prevent the machine from "walking" while leveling and provide a large bearing surface.

Color-coding the Change Parts

To facilitate quick changeovers, color-code the change parts. This also makes it easy to spot incorrect setups.

CAM AND DRIVE DESIGN

Considerations include:

• Camshaft support;
• Overload clutches;
• Compressible cam linkages;
• Replacement parts;
• Spare components;
• Belt tensioners;
• Avoid adjustable cams;
• Independent cams;
• Split cams;
• Air springs;
• Precision motions;
• Precision locating;
• Control motions;
• Backlash; and
• Gear backlash.

Camshaft Support

Always support camshafts with a bearing in the area of the cams to prevent the shaft from flexing under cam load. Shaft flexing reduces the motion at the work site.

Overload Clutches

Use overload clutches on line shafts, workstations, camshafts, and other items to avoid tooling damage in the event of a jam.

Compressible Cam Linkages

Use compressible links to transmit cam-generated motions. Links must be stiff enough to accomplish the task but compress during jams. Compressible links save tooling and prevent serious damage to the machine.

Replacement Parts

Any component subject to wear should be designed for quick replacement. Replacement due to wear is the same whether the wear occurs at one station or is spread among 50 fixtures. For example, replacing one fixture every 100,000 cycles is equivalent, in parts replaced per million cycles, to replacing 50 fixtures every 5,000,000 cycles. Designing for quick and accurate replacement is important in either case.

Spare Components

Design the machine so that timing belts can be replaced without removing bearings or other components. When this is not possible, place a spare timing belt or two on the machine so that the old one can just be cut, removed, and replaced with the spare, as shown in Figure A-2.

Belt Tensioners

Use belt tensioners on all belts.

Avoid Adjustable Cams

Avoid using adjustable timing on cams. Adjustable cams are put out of adjustment at some time. If you use an adjustable cam during startup, replace it with a keyed, nonadjustable cam prior to putting the machine into production.

Independent Cams

Independent cam motions (one cam for each motion) are generally the best.

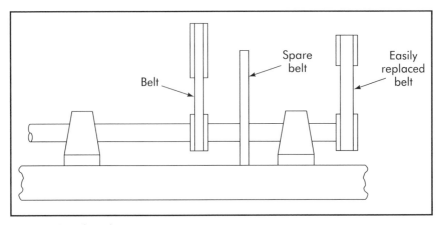

Figure A-2. Belt replacement.

Split Cams

Use split cams wherever possible to facilitate replacement or change.

Air Springs

Use air springs at the tooling end of the cam arms to provide adjustable force.

Precision Motions

On precision mechanisms, use a hard stop in the tooling to control the limit position of the mechanism. On cam-actuated machines, this requires a small over-travel on the cam motion and a compliant link in the system. Compliance of .02-.03 in. (0.5-0.8 mm) is typically enough.

Precision Locating

Use shot pins or kinematic alignment features for high precision tooling.

Control Motions

Control the kinematics (position, velocity, acceleration, jerk) at all times using cams, servos/steppers, or voice coils. Avoid air cylinders wherever possible.

Backlash

Backlash can often be eliminated if the mechanism is always torqued or driven in the same direction. This is easier to achieve with continuous motion devices.

Gear Backlash

To remove backlash in spur gears, split two gears in half through the diameter. Put threaded holes in one, slotted holes in the other, and bolt the two halves together. Offset the two halves slightly to remove any backlash with the mating gear. Some brands offer this feature on off-the-shelf items.

ADJUSTING/LOCATING/PHASING

Tips for adjusting, locating, and/or phasing involve:

- Avoiding unnecessary adjustments;
- Avoiding shims;
- Locating features;
- Fine adjustment; and
- Phase adjustment.

Avoid Unnecessary Adjustments

Avoid adjustments in production equipment. Determine the optimum setting during equipment qualification, and fix the positions in place with pins or other permanent means.

Avoiding Shims

Avoid use of shims; they get lost when removed. Design in spacers that are at least .25-in. (6.4-mm) thick and can be ground to correct thickness. When the use of shims is unavoidable, put shims in areas that are least likely to be disassembled. If possible, fasten shims in place and mark thickness and location.

Locating Features

Machine-in locating features (for example, keys, pockets, and so on) on mating parts instead of "drill and pin at assembly." This saves time during assembly and makes maintenance faster and easier. Figure A-3 and Figure A-4 show examples.

Fine Adjustment

For critical alignment where adjustments are required, design parts with fine adjustment features (for example, a fine-thread adjusting screw) and use a fixture at assembly for final positioning. This has the advantage of using less expensive parts, elimination of tolerance stackup, and easier realignment.

Phase Adjustment

Use phasers on all assembly machine workstations that run off a line shaft. Each station can then be adjusted to achieve maximum accuracy.

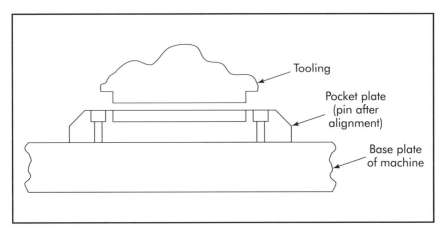

Figure A-3. Machined-in locating features.

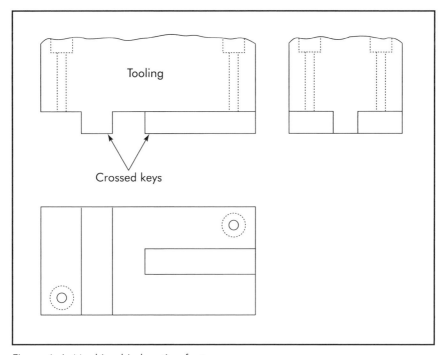

Figure A-4. Machined-in locating features.

Use infinite phase adjusters (harmonic) where machine phasing is required. The slight additional cost will be more than made up for during assembly and startup.

FASTENING

The tips provided on fastening involve socket-head cap screws, split collars versus setscrews, standardized fasteners, hardened washers, and bolt tensioning.

Socket-head Cap Screws

Don't use lock washers under socket-head cap screws. Eventually, lock washers cold-form and become loose. Use screws with self-locking inserts or thread-locking material if loosening is a concern.

Split Collars versus Setscrews

Avoid using setscrews to lock parts onto a shaft. Setscrews mar the shaft and make it more difficult to remove. Use split collars or similar clamping designs. Also, use clamp-type collars on shafts and ball bearing units, as shown in Figures A-5 and A-6.

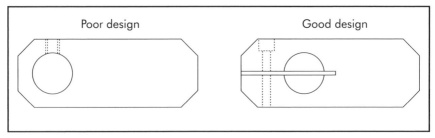

Figure A-5. Setscrew compared to a clamp.

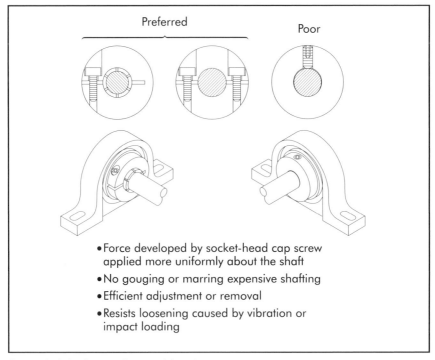

Figure A-6. Locking collars and bearings.

Standardized Fasteners

On a machine, standardize the types of fasteners (hex or socket head) and limit variation in sizes (diameters and length).

Hardened Washers

Use heavy-duty hardened washers in place of standard washers in most cases. They prevent damage to the parts and provide better clamping.

Bolt Tensioning

Assuming that a bolt and joint are designed adequately, if the bolt does not fail during wrenching, it won't fail in service. A bolt is subjected to both tension and torsion due to friction during wrenching. Only the tension remains after wrenching. A bolt must be properly "loaded" to remain tight. A bolt that is not torqued correctly does not have enough residual tension to remain tight. Longer bolts generally resist loosening and fatigue better than shorter bolts, because more residual tension remains after normal relaxation from deformation and cold-flow in the bearing surface.

MATERIALS AND COATINGS

Automation tips for materials and coatings focus on controlling cost and wear.

Material Cost

Use high-performance materials on critical parts. Since the cost of material is usually a small percentage of the total cost of making finished parts, use of aluminums and stainless steels offer many advantages worth considering. For aluminum machined parts, 7075-T651 is the strongest of the commercial aluminums. In fact, it is stronger than hot-rolled steel. For small steel parts, 15-5 precipitation hardenable (PH) or 17-4PH stainless steels should be used and heat-treated to the H900 (44 R_c [Rockwell Hardness Scale]) condition. Advantages include a good combination of high yield strength (up to 80,000 psi [552 MN]) and very low dimensional change during heat treating, possibly avoiding the need to machine the part after heat treating.

Wear Coating

Hard coating, such as Diamond Black™ coating (equivalent to 90-93 R_c), is recommended for wear areas where contact loading is low. Such coatings work best on hardened steel substrates.

Index

I

incoming materials and components, 21-22

incremental encoders, 160

indexing mechanisms, (fig. 5-4), 102, 104

initial cost compared to total cost, 177

ink cartridge design, (fig. 4-5), 83, (fig. 4-6), 84

in-line transfer (intermittent), 102

input/output (I/O) list, 44

inspection, 141

installation requirements, 43

integrating a new manufacturing system, (fig. 3-7), 65

interface requirements, 41

intermittent transfer methods, 99
    carousel, 105, (fig. 5-6), 107
    double-tooled carousel, (fig. 5-7), 108
    indexing mechanisms, 102
    in-line (precision link), (fig. 5-3), 102-103
    in-line (walking beam), (fig. 5-5), 105-106
    rotary, (fig. 5-2), 101

J

jackscrew
    and compression spring, (fig. 9-11), 194
    pair, (fig. 9-12), 194
    replaced with a threaded rod, (fig. 9-14), 195
    simple, (fig. 9-13), 194

jams
    downtime, (eq. 3-7), 59
    quick clearing of, 189

L

laser sensors, 162, (fig. 8-6), 163

leveling pads, 215

lighting, 144

linear vibratory feeder, (fig. 6-2), 126

linkage bearings, 214

locating features, machined-in, (figs. A-3 and A-4), 218

locking collars and bearings, (fig. A-6), 220

lubrication (central), 185

M

machine
    adjustments, 193
    capability (synchronous), (table 3-7), 73
    cleanup, 185
    controllers, 148
    downtime (%), (eq. 3-6), 58
    performance during debug, check-out, and startup, (fig. 10-1), 201
    speed increase and downtime, (tables 3-2 and 3-3), 60
    vision, 142

machined-in locating features, (figs. A-3 and A-4), 218

magazine feed, 132

magnetic latch, (fig. 9-9), 191

magnetostrictive
    sensors, 156
    solutions for roller gap control, (fig. 8-5), 159

maintenance and operator access, 185

manual, outline for new equipment, (table 10-1), 209

manufactured on-line, 133

manufacturing
    goals, 1
    information systems (MIS), 174
    stages, 1-3

marking parts, 214

materials and coatings, 221

math functions for cam design, (table 9-1), 182

measurement and visual inspection, 142

mechanical
    design influence on control, 196
    switches, 161

motion control, 165
    controllers, 148
    coordinated motion-electronic gearing, 169
    motors, 165-167
    servo motor drive, 167

motors
    AC induction, 165
    brushless AC, 166